THE YEAR 1000

Also by Robert Lacey

Robert, Earl of Essex
The Life and Times of Henry VIII
The Queens of the North Atlantic
Sir Walter Ralegh
Majesty: Elizabeth II and the House of Windsor
The Kingdom
Princess
Aristocrats
Ford: The Men and the Machine
Queen Mother
Little Man
Grace
Sotheby's — Bidding For Class

Also by Danny Danziger

The Happiness Book
All in a Day's Work
Eton Voices
The Noble Tradition
The Cathedral
Lost Hearts
The Orchestra

THE YEAR 1000

WHAT LIFE WAS LIKE AT THE TURN
OF THE FIRST MILLENNIUM

An Englishman's World

ROBERT LACEY

DANNY DANZIGER

LITTLE, BROWN AND COMPANY

A *Little, Brown* Book

First published in Great Britain in 1999
by Little, Brown and Company
Reprinted 1999 (nine times)

A CIP catalogue record for this book is
available from the British Library

ISBN 0 316 64375 0

Monthly chapter illustrations from the
Julius Work calendar, c. AD 1020, Canterbury Cathedral,
reproduced courtesy of the British Library

Printed and bound in Great Britain by
Clays Ltd, St Ives plc

Little, Brown and Company (UK)
Brettenham House
Lancaster Place
London WC2E 7EN

Contents

To our partners and colleagues at *Cover* magazine

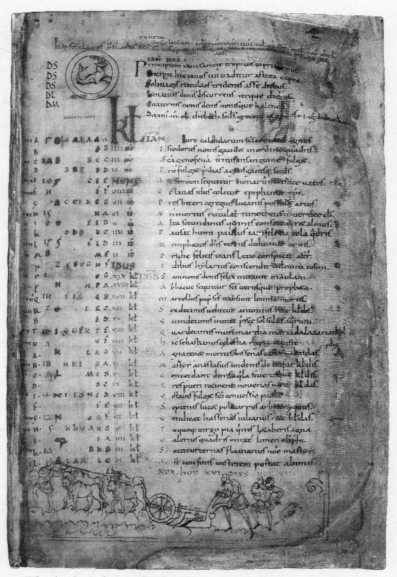

"The ploughman feeds us all." The January page from the Julius Work Calendar, produced in the writing studio of Canterbury Cathedral some time around AD 1020.

I warmly welcome your eager desire to know something of the doings and sayings of the great men of the past, and of our own nation, in particular.

— *The Venerable Bede (673–735)*

And some there be which have no memorial; who are perished as though they had never been; and are become as though they had never been born; and their children after them. But these were merciful men, whose righteousness hath not been forgotten.

— *Ecclesiasticus, chapter xliv, verse 9*

We dare not lengthen this book much more, lest it be out of moderation and should stir up men's antipathy because of its size.

— *Aelfric, schoolteacher of Cerne Abbas,*
later Abbot of Eynsham (c. 995–1020)

THE JULIUS WORK CALENDAR

The Wonder of Survival

❖ ❖ ❖

I T WAS AN OAK TREE THAT PROVIDED THE
ink, from a boil-like pimple growing out of its bark. A
wasp had gnawed into the wood to lay its eggs there,
and, in self-defence, the tree formed a gall round the intru-
sion, circular and hard-skinned like a crab apple, full of
clear acid. "Encaustum" was what they called ink in the year
1000, from the Latin *caustere*, "to bite," because the fluid from
the galls on an oak tree literally bit into the parchment,
which was flayed from the skin of lamb or calf or kid. Ink
was a treacly liquid in those days. You crushed the oak galls
in rainwater or vinegar, thickened it with gum arabic, then
added iron salts to colour the acid.

The colouring selected by this particular scribe has lent a
brownish tinge to his black ink, and the book itself is quite
small, no thicker or taller than any modern hardback on the
shelf. Touch its springy, still-velvety surface, and you are
touching history. You can almost smell it. You are in physical contact with something that was created nearly a thousand years ago, sometime around the year 1020, probably by
a cleric working in the manuscript studio at Canterbury
Cathedral.

This ancient document is known today as the Julius Work Calendar. With its combination of calendar calculation and impressionistic sketching (see frontispiece), it is the earliest surviving document of its sort in England, and it provides the basis of this modern book that you have picked up and are now reading a millennium later — an attempt to look back and discover what life was like in England in the year 1000. We owe the survival of the document to the seventeenth-century book collector Sir Robert Cotton, who retrieved it from the dispersal of manuscripts that followed Henry VIII's dissolution of the monasteries. Sir Robert stored the little volume in his grand Westminster library, where each bookcase was decorated with the bust of a Roman emperor — Tiberius, Augustus, Diocletian, Nero, Vespasian, Julius — and these resonant imperial names became the basis of the Cotton cataloguing system. Tiberius D. III indicated a book that was stacked on the shelf marked D, third volume along, below the bust of Tiberius, and our work calendar was stacked below the bust of Julius Caesar.[1]

At the time of writing, the Julius Work Calendar is preserved behind the fluted colonnades of the British Museum, but by the year 2000 it is destined to be transferred to the sparkling new British Library beside St. Pancras Station. In the course of the centuries, the calendar has lost the heavy wooden covers between which it was originally pressed to stop the vellum reverting to the shape of the animal from which it came. It bears the scratchings and scribblings of the generations — along with the scarrings of the old British Museum's once mandatory red stamp.

In layout it is curiously contemporary — twelve months

on twelve pages, each sheet headed with the name of that particular month and the sign of the zodiac. Its purpose was religious, to list the high days and holy days to be celebrated in church that month, probably as an instructional manual for young monks. Its 365 lines of Latin verse take the form of a sing-song doggerel which one can imagine the young oblates chanting as they were inducted into the rituals of the Christian year. In that sense, the calendar belongs to a world that is long vanished, but in spirit and appearance it is not that different from a twelve-page calendar hanging on the wall of a modern kitchen.

Here is the earliest surviving example of an Englishman laying out life in a daily routine, juggling time, the schedule of the earth, and the life of the spirit. The days of the month are listed down the page, below that month's sign of the zodiac, and across the bottom of each sheet runs a delicate little drawing which illustrates the task of the month — a bearded ploughman following the oxen, shepherds gossiping while they watch over their sheep, two men reaping in harmony while another takes a rest. The artist's line is lithe and sprightly, depicting real human beings, not puppets. The figures have muscles and potbellies, bald heads, warts and frowns — joys and worries. These are people like us.

Modern English history conventionally begins in 1066 with the arrival of William the Conqueror and the Normans, but we are going back before that, to late Anglo-Saxon England, where the cheerful and sturdy characters of the Julius Work Calendar open the door to a world which is both alien and curiously familiar. So welcome to the year 1000, and *Lege Feliciter*, as the Venerable Bede once put it: May you read happily![2]

JANUARY

FOR ALL THE SAINTS

I F YOU WERE TO MEET AN ENGLISHMAN IN
the year 1000, the first thing that would strike you
would be how tall he was — very much the size of anyone alive today.[3] It is generally believed that we are taller
than our ancestors, and that is certainly true when we com-
pare our stature to the size of more recent generations.
Malnourished and overcrowded, the inhabitants of Geor-
gian or Victorian England could not match our health or
physique at the end of the twentieth century.

But the bones that have been excavated from the graves of
people buried in England in the years around 1000 tell a tale
of strong and healthy folk — the Anglo-Saxons who had
occupied the greater part of the British Isles since the
departure of the Romans. Nine out of ten of them lived in a
green and unpolluted countryside on a simple, wholesome
diet that grew sturdy limbs — and very healthy teeth. It
was during the centuries that followed the first millennium
that overpopulation and overcrowding started to affect the
stature and well-being of western Europeans. Excavations
of later medieval sites reveal bodies that are already smaller
than those discovered from the years around 1000, and

archaeologists who have studied these centuries say that they can almost see the devastation of the Black Death looming in the evidence of the increasingly frail and unhealthy skeletal remains.[4]

Life was simple. People wore the simple, sack-like tunics with leggings that we laugh at in the Monty Python movies, though in colours that were rather less muddy. Despite the lack of sharp chemical dyes in the year 1000, natural vegetable colourings could produce a range of strong and cheerful hues, with bright reds, greens, and yellows. It was a world without buttons, which had yet to be invented. Clothes were still fastened with clasps and thongs.

Life was short. A boy of twelve was considered old enough to swear an oath of allegiance to the king, while girls got married in their early teens, often to men who were significantly older than they were. Most adults died in their forties, and fifty-year-olds were considered venerable indeed. No one "went out to work," but the evidence of arthritis in the bones excavated from Anglo-Saxon graves indicates that most people endured a lifetime of hard manual labour — and the Julius Work Calendar shows the different forms which that labour could take. Across the bottom of January's calendar page moves the ploughman, slicing open England's damp and often clay-ridden crust with the heavy iron blade that had been the making of the country's farming landscape.

"The ploughman feeds us all," declared Aelfric, the Wessex schoolmaster who, in the years 987 to 1002, taught his pupils by getting them to observe and analyse the different economic activities they could see around them. "The ploughman gives us bread and drink."[5]

It looks so slow and primitive to us, the heavy plough dragged by the oxen train. But compared to farming technologies in many other parts of the world at that time, the wheeled and iron-bladed plough of northwestern Europe was supercharged, enabling just two men to tear up a whole acre of soil with the help of the beasts which not only provided the "horsepower," but enriched the fields with their manure.

The wheeled plough was the foundation of life for English people living in the year 1000. It opened the soil to air and water, enabling soluble minerals to reach deep levels, while rooting out weeds and tossing them aside to wither in the open air. It was not a new invention. In the middle of the first century A.D., the Roman historian Pliny the Elder described some such device in use to the north of the Alps, and the evidence suggests that this powerful and handy machine was the crucial element in cultivating the land cleared from Europe's northwestern forests.[6] One man to hold the plough, one to walk with the oxen, coaxing and singing and, when necessary, goading the animals forward with a stick: this drawing shows the furrows of freshly turned earth, the secret of how the soil had been tamed in the course of the previous centuries. It was the reason why, by the turn of the millennium, England was able to support a population of at least a million souls.

The calendar page on which the wheeled plough was sketched represented an equally developed and practical technology — the measuring of time. Today we take calendars for granted. Garages hand them out for nothing at Christmas. But the challenge of how to formulate a working system of dates had consumed the energies of the brightest minds for centuries, with every culture and religion devising its own system of reckoning, and in Christendom confusion centred particularly on the timing of the Church's most important festival — Easter.

The early Christians debated it furiously. Christ was crucified as the Jews gathered in Jerusalem for the feast of Passover, so Easter's timing depended on the Jewish lunar calendar based on the 29½-day cycle from new moon to new moon. But planning a full year's sequence of church festivals meant that the lunar timetable had to be fitted into the 365¼-day rotation of the seasons, based on the annual cycle of the sun — and whichever way you try to squeeze it, 29½ into 365¼ does not go.

"Such was the confusion in those days," related the Venerable Bede, the great chronicler of the times, describing the calendar arguments in mid-seventh-century England, "that Easter was sometimes kept twice in one year, so that when the King had ended Lent and was keeping Easter, the Queen and her attendants were still fasting and keeping Palm Sunday."[7]

The king was Oswy of Northumbria, the northernmost of the early Anglo-Saxon kingdoms. Oswy followed the calendar of the Irish-influenced monks of Lindisfarne, who first converted Northumbria, while his bride, Eanfled of Kent, stayed true to the Roman calculations with which she had been brought up in Canterbury. A learned synod was convened at Whitby on the Yorkshire coast to resolve this and several other conflicts of church practice, and it provoked deep ill-humour.

"Easter is observed by men of different nations and languages at one and the same time in Africa, Asia, Egypt,

Greece, and throughout the world," argued Canterbury's representative. "The only people who stupidly contend against the whole world are those Irishmen and their partners in obstinacy, the Picts and Britons, who inhabit only a portion of these, the two uppermost islands of the ocean."[8]

"It is strange that you call us stupid," retorted the Irish delegation, citing the Apostle John as their authority. They set out their own system of juggling the moon and sun cycles with all the disdainful superiority of the senior faith, since the Irish had been Christians long before the English. St. Patrick had established his church in Ireland a century and a half before Pope Gregory's envoy Augustine arrived in Canterbury to found the English church, and it had been missionaries from Ireland, not Kent, who had Christianised Scotland and the north of England.

But when the seaside convention concluded its arguments, it was Canterbury that won the day — a victory, in terms of church politics, for the centralising authority of the Pope in Rome, and a decision, in terms of the calendar, that opened the way for Bede, the monk from Tyneside who was both historical chronicler and master mathematician, to work out a system of dating that would settle the argument once and for all.

On the eve of the year 2000, the English have staked a proprietorial interest in the turning of the second millennium, thanks to Greenwich with its mean time and the zero line of longitude. Thanks to the Venerable Bede, they could claim a similar interest in the first. Not that we should look for Domes or any special millennarial monuments in 1000 A.D. It was an anniversary which, by definition, could only mean something to people who dated their history from the birth of Jesus, and even inside Christendom there were varying interpretations of that. But if any country worked to dates we would recognise today, it was England, and that was because of the Venerable Bede, who popularised the use of the Anno Domini system through his famous work *De Temporum Ratione*, "On the Reckoning of Time."

Composed in 725 A.D., *De Temporum Ratione* was based on the Easter calculations of the sixth-century Scythian scholar Dionysius Exiguus (Dennis the Little). In the course of compiling Easter tables for Pope John I, Dionysius had remarked, almost incidentally, how inappropriate it was for the Church to rely upon the pagan calendar of the Romans,[9] particularly since its years dated back to the great persecutor of the Christians, the Emperor Diocletian. Would it not make more sense, Dionysius had suggested, to date the Christian era from the birth of our Saviour Himself, which could be designated as the year 1?

The scholar made two major errors at this point. The concept of zero had not yet entered Western mathematical thinking, which operated in Roman numerals, so Dionysius's Christian era missed out the twelve months of year 0 needed to get to the start of year 1. Still more seriously, the year that Dionysius selected for Christ's birth actually fell four years after the death of the notorious King Herod, who had been so memorably enraged by the birth in Bethlehem of a rival king of the Jews. The Gospel description of Christ's birth as occurring in the reign of Herod means that Jesus was probably born in 4 B.C., or even earlier (which also means that the second millennium of his birth should actually have been celebrated in 1996 or 1997, and not in the year 2000).

Bede detected this error in Dionysius's proposed year 1 A.D., but evidently felt that the few years of inaccuracy mattered less than the dazzling concept of dating history according to the "Years of Grace," the era of Christ's reign on earth. When Bede composed his great *Ecclesiastical History of the English People* in 731, he used the Anno Domini dating system, and when, at the end of the next century, the scribes of the *Anglo-Saxon Chronicle* started their work of recording England's history year by year, it was Bede's system that they followed.

Confusion remained as to what day was the true beginning of the Christian year. Bede took it for granted that the year should begin with the birth of Christ himself, on December 25. But following that logic back through nine months of pregnancy, one arrived at March 25, the Feast of the Annunciation, or Lady Day, the festival celebrated by the church in commemoration of Mary's visitation from the Angel Gabriel, and the news that she was bearing the Christ child. For a Christian this represented the earliest manifestation of the Divine Presence on earth, and Lady Day was accordingly celebrated for centuries as the true beginning of the year. As late as the 1660s, Samuel Pepys reflected this enduring confusion in his *Diaries*, starting his reckoning of the years on Lady Day (March 25), but also noting the Roman consular date of January 1 as "New Year's Day."

All this complicated grappling with the imponderables of sun, moon, stars, and the fallible accretions of human history is graphically displayed on the pages of the Julius Work Calendar, which takes the twelve Roman months with which we today are familiar, and overlays them with a filigree of Christian elaboration. The mysterious-looking columns of letters and numerals that run down the left-hand side of every page are part of the mechanism for calculating Easter and other festivals. The so-called Golden numbers indicate the occurrence of the new moon, while the Dominical letters show where Sundays will fall in any given year — since this calendar does not relate to one particular set of twelve months. It is a perpetual calendar, and its complicated codings are like the innards of a computer, baffling to the layman, but the route to knowledge for those who understand the code.

One inch in from the left of the page runs a solid column of Roman numerals setting out the day of the month according to the Romans' own daunting system of counting things backwards — from KL, the Kalends, or first day of the month, down through the Nones to the Ides, the turning point of the month, which fell on the thirteenth or fifteenth. But it is the writing to the right of the date that really matters, for here was listed the main purpose of the calendar, the names of the saints and religious festivals to be observed.

Good and evil were living companions to people in the year 1000. When someone was said to have the Devil in him, people took it quite literally. Jack Frost was not "weather" to people who had to survive without central heating through a damp medieval winter. He was mischief personified — a kinsman of the Devil, nipping noses and fingers, making the ground too hard to work. He was one of a legion of little people, elves and trolls and fairies, who inhabited the fears and imaginings of early medieval folk.

But the Church had its own army of spirits, the saints who had lived their lives — and often lost their lives — for the sake of Jesus' teaching, and the principal purpose of the Julius Work Calendar was to provide a daily diary of encounters with those holy folk whose lives were an example and promise of how things could get better. This was the spiritual function of the calendar, and at a more basic level it provided a guide through a wonderfully varied collection of human characters whose lives, adventures, and personalities provided entertainment, as close as any medieval document could get to gossip.

Personal portraits did not really exist in the early Middle Ages. Even kings were only depicted as symbolic and idealised figures on their coins. But when it came to the lives of the saints, you had a chance to analyse their personalities, pondering the peculiarities of a character like Simeon Stylites, the fifth-century hermit who spent much of his life living naked on top of increasingly high pillars, or learning from the life of Mary of Egypt, the patron saint of fallen women. Mary was an Egyptian who left home at the age of twelve and went to live in fifth-century Alexandria, where she became a prostitute for seventeen years. Through curiosity she joined a pilgrimage to Jerusalem, paying for her passage by offering herself to the sailors. But on arriving at the holy city with her fellow pilgrims, she found it impossible to enter the church. She felt herself held back by an invisible force, and when she lifted her eyes to an image of the Virgin Mary, she heard a voice telling her to cross the river Jordan, where she would find rest. So, according to legend, she bought three loaves and went to live in the desert, spending the rest of her life there living on dates and berries. When her clothes wore out, her hair grew long enough to cover her modesty, and she dedicated the rest of her life to prayer and contemplation. Mary featured frequently in medieval chronicles and church statues, identified by her long hair and by the three loaves that became her emblem.[10]

People identified with the personalities and quirks of saints, as today they feel they know soap opera stars. The hagiographies that recounted their stories were bland and stereotyped eulogies, usually written by loyal followers and friends. But human clues lurked in the details, and every saint's day of the month offered its own drama. In the monasteries, morning prayers were said to that day's holy figures. Prayer was a way of asking a saint to pay attention to your own particular worries. Singing was a beautiful way of saying, "Please listen." The God of the Middle Ages was a God who intervened actively in daily life. That was the message of the miracles executed by Jesus and continued by his saints. So one function of worship was to secure divine intervention on your own behalf.

After prime, the first service of the day after sunrise, the monks would repair to their chapterhouse — the monastery meeting room — where the lives of that day's saints would be read out, and one of the sermons preached in chapel might well take an incident from the life of that particular day's saint as the jumping-off point for some practical teaching.[11] January 5 offered the feast day of Simeon Stylites, the pillar-dwelling hermit, while other days featured Isidorus of Seville, who had proclaimed that there

should be a cathedral school in every diocese; St. Gene-
vieve, who saved Paris from Attila the Hun, and whose candle was blown out by the devil when she went to pray at
night; St. Lucien, who was imprisoned for his faith by the
emperor Diocletian; St. Timothy, a companion of St. Paul
who was stoned to death by the heathens; St. Secundinus,
who wrote the earliest known Latin hymn in Ireland; and
the hermit St. Paul of Thebes, who was said to have survived more than a hundred years of piety and austerity in
the desert.

Each hero or heroine had their own lesson to teach.
It could carry you through the day, a psychic talisman of
encouragement, and the geography of the saints' adventures — from Antioch to Seville, then north to Paris and
Ireland — provided a lesson in itself about the varied shape
and character of a world which extended further than we
might imagine. The Anglo-Saxons knew of three conti-
nents — Europe, Africa, and Asia — and they also knew
about India. Late in the ninth century King Alfred sent
money to help the Christian missionaries there.

England itself was a network of magical sites. The altar of
every church contained the physical relics of at least one
saint. The origin of the tradition whereby many modern
churches are dedicated to a particular saint goes back to the
founding principle of Roman church belief that a saint is
intimately present wherever his or her relics might rest.
Heaven was visualised as being something like the royal
court. God sat there in judgement like the king, and paid
most attention to those who could catch His ear. On earth
it was the great warriors and magnates who enjoyed that
access. In heaven it was the saints. Their holy lives and

suffering on earth had earned them direct transfer from earth to God's presence, without any waiting in purgatory, while their bodies, or the body parts reposing in the altar of their church, were believed to be still living. Many were the reports of saints' tombs being opened and evidences of life being discovered — growing hair or nails, or unperished limbs still containing blood — proof of the vitality and effectiveness of the Christian god. The churches whose saints proved particularly potent became centres of cults and pilgrimage.

When King Ethelbert of Kent received the first group of Christian priests who brought him greetings from the Pope in Rome in 597 A.D., he insisted on meeting them in the open air, so the wind would blow away any spells that they might try to cast upon him with their alien magic.[12] Four hundred years later the Christian magic had all England in its thrall, and the shrines of its saints provided the nation with its energy centres. Up in the north were the relics of the Venerable Bede, cherished since his death in 735 by the monks of Tyneside and Wear. Within fifty years of his death his cult as a saint was well established by local testimony that his relics had worked miraculous cures, and the potency of Bede's bones was such that many laid claim to them. In the mid-eleventh century they were transferred to Durham. Down in Wessex, Glastonbury claimed some relics of Bede to augment the abbey's reputation as one of the most holy spots in England. According to later legend, Jesus himself had walked in ancient times at Glastonbury "in England's pleasant pastures," and St. Joseph of Arimethea had travelled here to plant the famous Glastonbury

Thorn, which had been taken from the Crown of Christ, and which flowered every year at Christmas.[13]

At the heart of Wessex, in the great cathedral at Winchester, lay the body of St. Swithin, bishop of Winchester in the middle of the ninth century, and the object of a busy cult within a century of his death. According to Aelfric, the schoolteacher and great prose writer of his day, the sick flocked to Winchester in vast numbers to be cured by St. Swithin. "Within ten days," recorded Aelfric, "two hundred men were healed, and so many within twelve months, that no man could count them. The burial ground lay filled with crippled folk, so that one could not easily visit the cathedral."[14]

Aelfric was a teacher in the monastery school in Cerne Abbas, a few days' ride from Winchester, where he himself was educated, so it seems most likely that he was reporting from firsthand observation. Living and teaching for more than a dozen years in the shadow of the Cerne Abbas giant, the great pagan fertility god with rampant genitalia carved out of the chalk hillside above the village, it is not surprising that the ironic and quizzical Aelfric should have displayed a detached view of certain human claims to contact with the supernatural: "Some dreams are in truth from God, even as we read in books," he once wrote, "and some are from the Devil for some deceit, seeking how he may pervert the soul." But of the miracles in the crowded tenth-century cemetery of Winchester, Aelfric had no doubt: "All were so miraculously healed within a few days," he wrote, "that one could not find there five unsound men out of that great crowd."[15]

This was an age of faith. People believed as fervently in

the powers of saints' bones as many today believe that wheat bran or jogging or psychoanalysis can increase the sum of human happiness. The saints had lived real lives. They had measured their principles fearlessly against adversity — and many had lived quite recently, since there was no formal process of canonisation as there is today. A beloved local abbot or abbess could become a saint in their locality within a few years of their death. Mass outpourings of grief like that which attended the death of Diana, Princess of Wales, in 1997 were the first step to sainthood in the year 1000. The next step was the testimony of the faithful to portents and miracles occurring.

You were not on your own. That was the comforting message of the little Julius Work Calendar with its twelve monthly recitations of saints' festivals. God was there to help, and so was a whole network of fellow human beings, from the distant past up to your own era. In the year 1000 the saints were a presence as vital and dynamic as any band of elves or demons. They were a living community to whom one prayed, and among whom one lived.

FEBRUARY

WELCOME TO ENGLA-LOND

I T IS TIME TO MEET SOMEONE FROM THE
year 1000 — at least to the extent that dry, legal documents can provide human contact across the years.
Here is Aelfflaed, a noblewoman who died some time
between 1000 and 1002, leaving huge estates in Essex and
East Anglia.[16] Here is Wulfgeat of Donnington in Shrop-
shire, a more modest landowner with estates that he
bequeathed to his wife and daughter.[17] And here is the charitable Bishop Aelfwold of Crediton in the West Country,
who died in 1008, anxious to free all the slaves who had
worked on his estates.[18]

We know about Aelfflaed, Wulfgeat, and Bishop Aelfwold from their wills, and, by the nature of wills, we know
more about their material possessions than we can discover
about their personal, spiritual lives. But Aelfflaed's will tells
us that she had supervised the farming of many acres with
apparent success, giving orders to men in a male-dominated
society, while Wulfgeat of Donnington clearly found nothing unusual in leaving his lands to be run by his womenfolk. There are no women depicted on the Julius Work

Calendar, but, as we will see, women who possessed sufficient strength of character were able to claim power and
exercise authority in the England of the year 1000. One
would expect a bishop to leave some pious bequests, but
Aelfwold's will lets us know that there was slave labour in
Anglo-Saxon England — while suggesting that people felt
uneasy enough about the fact to free slaves when they
passed on to another life. The dry legal documents that
have survived a millennium provide only clues, but with
their help, and with other sources of evidence, we can start
to creep a little way, at least, into real minds and hearts.

Skull measurements show that the brain capacity of a
man or woman living in the year 1000 was exactly the same
as our own.[19] These were not people we should patronise.
They were practical, self-contained folk, not given to excessive agonising or self-analysis, to judge from the few who
committed their thoughts to paper — the ideal type to
choose as companions on a desert island, since they were
skilful with their hands, and they could turn their hands to
anything. They knew how to make and mend, and when
their day's work was done, they could also be very good
company, since one of the most important things they had
learned in their lives was how to entertain themselves. The
knowledge in their heads had rarely come directly from
books — only a small minority of them could read — and
they retained the data without the help of filing cabinets or
mechanical storage systems. They had learned everything
by observing and imitating, usually by standing alongside
an adult who was almost certainly their father or mother,
and by memorising everything they needed to survive and
enrich their lives.

Their poetry and stories were only just beginning to be written down. The Anglo-Saxons learned most of their folklore by heart. They could tell long, complicated tales of their family histories — who begat whom, back to when their ancestors had first arrived in England from the forests beyond the sea. And they loved to recite their ancient folk poems by heart — violent and bloodthirsty sagas of wild beasts and warriors, which retained the echo of the voyages that had brought their forefathers to the "outermost islands" on the edge of the great ocean.

The poet Robert Graves remarked on how the heave-ho of Old English poetry sounded like rowing, with the rhythm of the verse recalling the dip and drag of oars back and forth, and certainly the great Anglo-Saxon epic *Beowulf*, reciting an ancient story and surviving in a book that was written around the year 1000 itself, came to special life when describing a sea journey:

> *Over the waves, with the wind behind her*
> *And foam at her prow, she flew like a bird*
> *Until her curved neck had covered the distance*
> *And on the following day, just when they hoped to,*
> *Those seafarers sighted land,*
> *Sunlit cliffs, sheer crags*
> *And looming headlands, the landfall they sought.*[20]

Beowulf (translated here by Seamus Heaney) was unusual for being written down, which makes it particularly precious evidence — like the Julius Work Calendar. February's calendar drawing shows a vigorous yard of vines getting pruned, a process which, by tradition, started on St. Vincent's Day, January 22.[21] As with the depiction of ploughing in January, the sketching of this apparently routine agricultural process was heavy with meaning, since the purpose of pruning is to direct the growth energies of a plant into the channels desired by the cultivator. It is all about human control — a well-pruned plant yields more than a wild one. So just as the wheeled plough embodied millennial man's mastery of the soil, the skilful pruning of branches demonstrated his ability to create a profitable working partnership with God's bushes, vines, and trees.

The plant limbs writhe and twist almost threateningly in this particular labour of the month. Bursting with Jack-and-the-Beanstalk vigour, the vines seem imbued with as much life as the men who are tending them. But the cultivators maintain their control, thanks to their *serps*, the long, flat blades of iron, like hand-held ploughshares, that embodied their capacity to shape their environment — and it is the modern English landscape which provides the most enduring physical evidence of what the men and women of the year 1000 did with their lives. The Anglo-Saxons placed their imprint indelibly on the shape of the English countryside. By the year 1000, most of the towns and villages of modern England had been settled by the seafarers, who turned out to be good settlers and farmers. And their still more widespread legacy was the language that they spoke — a tongue of extreme strength, simplicity, and richness which has proved to be the primary foundation of how millions all over the globe today speak and think and frame their ideas.

The English language arrived in England, it has been said, on the point of a sword — and it arrived twice. Its first invasion was with the Angles, Saxons, Jutes, and other tribes of northern Holland and Germany who crossed the North Sea in the years after 450 to fill the vacuum left by the departing Romans. They were robust and determined aggressors — "warriors eager for fame," according to the *Anglo-Saxon Chronicle*, "proud war-smiths" who were relatives of the same German "barbarians" who had headed south to get involved in both sides of the battles over Rome (many Germans fought as mercenaries on the side of Rome). They experienced little difficulty in assimilating the friendly British and they drove those who were recalcitrant back into Cornwall, Wales, Scotland, and Ireland — the western crescent of windswept moors and mountains which has been called the Celtic fringe.[22] Between 450 and 600 the Anglo-Saxons took over most of the area which corresponds to modern England, and they referred to the dispossessed Britons as *wealisc*, meaning "foreign" — from which we get the word *Welsh*.

To the dispossessed Celts, the Germanic invaders were all Saxons — from which comes the Scottish word of abuse *Sassenach*. But many of the new arrivals started to classify themselves as Angles. Bede took up the word, describing them as *gens Anglorum*, and their language became known as *Englisc* (Angle-ish) — a tongue that was spoken to a rhythm and contained many words which we can recognise today without understanding a single thing. They organised themselves into a collection of small kingdoms, from Northumbria in the north, down through Mercia, which occupied roughly the area of the modern Midlands, while the south of the country was split between East Anglia, Kent, Essex, Sussex, and Wessex (the kingdoms of the East Saxons, South Saxons, and West Saxons).

Computer analysis of the English language as spoken today shows that the hundred most frequently used words are all of Anglo-Saxon origin: *the, is, you* — the basic building blocks.[23] When Winston Churchill wanted to rally the nation in 1940, it was to Anglo-Saxon that he turned: "We shall fight on the beaches; we shall fight on the landing grounds; we shall fight in the fields and the streets; we shall fight in the hills; we shall never surrender." All these stirring words came from Old English as spoken in the year 1000, with the exception of the last one, *surrender,* a French import that came with the Normans in 1066 — and when man set foot on the moon in 1969, the first human words spoken had similar echoes: "One small step for a man, one giant leap for mankind." Each of Neil Armstrong's famous words was part of Old English by the year 1000.

Perhaps this is also the place to remark that many of the earthy epithets often described as "Anglo-Saxon" did not arrive until comparatively recent times: *fokkinge, cunte, crappe,* and *bugger* were all much later imports, probably coming from Holland as the later Middle Ages shaded into the great age of seafaring and exploration. There are absolutely no swear words or obscenities in Anglo-Saxon English, at least as the language has come down to us in the documents composed by its monkish scribes. The Anglo-Saxons could swear *to do* something, or could swear *by* something, but there is no record of them swearing *at* anything at all.

When St. Augustine and his Christian missionaries arrived in 597 A.D. to turn the Angles into angels, *Englisc* proved remarkably flexible and welcoming to the terminology of the new religion. The word *angel* itself, along with *dis-*

ciple, martyr, relic, and *shrine* are just a few of the Greek and Latin words that were happily assimilated into the language. But the invasion that made the decisive contribution to the language was a second wave of Scandinavian trespassers — the Vikings who began to occupy the northern and eastern areas of England in the aftermath of raids that started in the 790s. This new generation of sea warriors came from the same corner of the North Sea as the original Anglo-Saxon invaders, and they spoke a very similar language. In the course of the next century the Vikings managed to overrun Northumbria, Mercia, East Anglia, and Essex. Only Wessex held the line against the fearsome Norsemen, whom the English referred to as "Danes" — and this was thanks to Wessex's remarkable young king, Alfred, who came to the throne in 871 after the death of his three elder brothers.

The famous tale of Alfred burning the cakes because he was worrying so much about how to defeat the Vikings entered English folklore in a document written around the year 1000. This would suggest that Alfred was the Winston Churchill of the English at the turn of the first millennium — or, more precisely, perhaps, their George Washington, since Alfred's retreat with a small band of followers into the swampy refuge of the Somerset marshes resonates with Washington's historic wintering in Valley Forge. The fate of Englishness hung on Alfred and his little band of stalwarts on the fortified island of Athelney. That was where legend had it that he burned the cakes which a farmer's wife had asked him to watch — they were probably lumps of dough set out on a griddle pan, over an open fire — and the king's brooding had fruitful consequences, for not only did he emerge from the marshes with a military strategy which repulsed the Vikings; he also devised an inspirational array of reforms and innovations that were to give decisive identity to the country that was by now known as "Engla-lond."

By the year 1000 Alfred had been dead for a century, but he ranked alongside the Venerable Bede as a shaper of England's developing identity. His greatest inspiration had been to understand how knowledge liberates — that knowledge is power. "The saddest thing about any man, is that he be ignorant," he once said, "and the most exciting thing is that he *knows*." Itching with intellectual and techno-logical curiosity, the king was anxious to work out the exact time of day. So he invented a graduated candle on which you could mark off the hours as it burned — and then, because his palaces were so draughty, he devised a venti-lated cow's horn lantern to put over the top and stop the candle blowing out. At the age of nearly forty, in the midst of what he described as "the various and manifold cares of his kingdom," Alfred started to learn Latin so that he could translate some of the key Latin texts into English. "It seems better to me . . . ," he wrote, "that we should translate certain books which are most necessary for all men to know into the language that we can all understand, and also arrange it . . . so that all the youth of free men now among the English people . . . are able to read English writing as well."

The king commissioned scholars to do most of the work, but he checked everything they wrote, and interspersed their translation with his own comments and musings in what was probably a sort of running seminar. He was an extraordinary inspiration, the only English monarch ever to be accorded the title "The Great," and the greatest achievement of his reign was the creation of the first history of England in the English language, the *Anglo-Saxon Chronicle*. By the year 1000 the *Chronicle* had been running just over a century, the work of monks in monasteries as far apart as Canterbury, Winchester, Worcester, and Peterborough.

In the military and political spheres, Alfred's achievement was to regain control of Wessex and to start on the capturing of the rest of Engla-lond. Within a few decades of his death in 899, the English writ ran all across southern England and far up into the Midlands, with the Norsemen driven back into the north and east of the country, inside an area that became known as the "Danelaw." The boundary between the original Anglo-Saxons and this second wave of newcomers roughly followed the line of Watling Street, the old Roman road that ran diagonally across the country from London to Chester. But many English remained living in the Danelaw, and as they dealt, day-by-day, with the invaders whose language was both similar yet awkwardly different from their own, the first and most important variety of "pidgin" English was developed.

Before the Viking invasions, both *Englisc* and Norse were strongly inflected languages, with the complicated grammatical word endings that persist to this day in German and, to a lesser extent, in French. If an Anglo-Saxon from Wessex wanted to say to someone in the Danelaw, "Have you a horse to sell?" he would ask, "*Haefst thu hors to sellenne?*" — which would correspond to "*Hefir thu hross at selja?*" in Norse. The Norseman would reply, "*Ek hefi tvau hors enn einn er aldr*" — meaning "I have two horses, but one is old," the equivalent of "*Ic haebbe tu hors ac an is eald*" in *Englisc*. The two men understood the important words — "*hors*" and "*hross*," "*eald*" and "*aldr*" — but they had difficulties when they came to their clashing grammar.[24]

The solution was the rubbing away through day-to-day usage of complicated word endings. Today most modern English plurals are formed simply by adding an *s* — one horse, two horses — and adjectives remain the same whether singular or plural. Nor are nouns divided between masculine and feminine, as they are in German, French, Spanish, Italian — and in every other European language. Norse also added extra flexibility to English, extending the range of verbal alternatives: you can *rear* (English) or *raise* (Norse) a child, and impart subtle distinctions to your meaning by choosing between *wish* (E) and *want* (N), *craft* (E) and *skill* (N), or *hide* (E) and *skin* (N).[25] By the year 1000, a hybrid language had been stirred together by the integration of the two great waves of invaders, and a common tongue existed that was at least roughly understood in every corner of the country.

Language helped and reflected political unification. By a canny combination of marriage alliances and battle, Alfred's children and grandchildren extended their authority into the Danelaw in the early tenth century until they controlled every corner of what we would recognise today as England. After Athelstan, shrewdest of the great king's grandsons, had himself crowned at Kings-ton (King's town), the modern Kingston-on-Thames, in 925 A.D., he grandiosely took to calling himself "King of all Britain," and he confirmed his authority, over England at least, by defeating an invading force of Scots and Irish in a bloodthirsty battle which the *Anglo-Saxon Chronicle* celebrated with a burst of Beowulfian verse:

> *The field darkened*
> *with soldiers' blood, after the morning-time*
> *when the sun, that glorious star,*
> *bright candle of God, the Lord eternal,*
> *glided over the depths . . .*
> *They left behind to divide the corpses,*
> *to enjoy the carrion, the dusty-coated,*
> *horny-beaked black raven,*
> *and the grey-coated eagle, white-rumped,*
> *greedy war-hawk, and the wolf,*
> *grey beast in the forest.*[26]

In the years following Athelstan's death in 939, the *Chronicle* recorded events great and small that made up the history of the now unified Engla-lond. In 962 A.D. there was "a very great pestilence" and "a great fatal fire" in London in which St. Paul's, the city's principal church, was burnt down — and then, in 973 A.D., King Edgar, Alfred's great-grandson, was anointed in Bath in a solemn coronation using a liturgy that remains the basis of English coronations to this day. If Archbishop Dunstan or any of the clergy officiating in Bath had found themselves in Westminster Abbey in 1953, they would have had little difficulty picking their way through the rituals of the coronation ceremony of Queen Elizabeth II.

In the year 978 A.D. the *Chronicle* recorded a tragi-comic accident in Wiltshire, where the royal council, almost to a man, fell through the floor of a newly constructed royal manor house at Calne, with the loss of several lives. It was an important entry in the history of English architecture, since it provides the earliest written evidence of a dwelling that was more than one storey high. Certain advances in construction techniques clearly remained to be worked out. But the *Chronicle* felt it significant to note that while some of England's doughtiest secular figures fell flailing to the floor, "the holy archbishop Dunstan alone was left standing up on a beam."[27]

Before leaving the month of February, let us spare a nod for Valentinus — the third-century priest who was martyred in Rome in the reign of the Emperor Claudius and whose feast day was celebrated on February 14, as it has been ever since. The details of St. Valentine's life are obscure, and ecclesiastical experts have been unable to discover any reason why he should have become the patron saint of lovers and romance. Historians note that mid-February was the occasion of the licentious Roman fertility festival of Lupercalia, when women sought cures for sterility, while folklorists trace the modern orgy of card-sending and candle-lit dinners back to the old country belief that birds commence coupling on February 14. Either or both of these explanations may be correct, and they would seem to illustrate the cleverness with which the early church appropriated heathen superstitions for its own purposes. But there is no Christian reason why St. Valentine should be the only saint in the calendar whose feast is celebrated with universal ardour today.

MARCH

HEADS FOR FOOD

NOWADAYS WE TALK ABOUT THE MAN OR woman in the street. In the year 1000 the average was represented by the man with the spade — or, in this month's calendar illustration, the man with the rake, the mattock, or pick-axe, and the apron full of seeds. The cultivator and his family were the backbone of the land.

The month of March heralded the arrival of spring. Winter was finally loosening its grip, for March was the month which contained the spring equinox. March 21 was the magical day blessed with exactly the same amount of light and dark in the course of twenty-four hours — and this is indicated by two sets of Roman numerals at the bottom of the calendar: NOX HOR XII (Night hours 12); HABET DIES HOR XII (The day has 12 hours). In January the calendar had listed sixteen hours of night and only eight of daylight, and for February the figures had been fourteen to ten. But from March 21 onwards the sun would annexe more and more of the night, and the cycle of cultivation could get seriously under way.

It was the quietness of life in a medieval English village

that would most strike a visitor from today — no planes overhead, no swish or rumble from traffic. Stop reading this book a minute. Can you hear something? Some machine turning? A waterpipe running? A distant radio or a pneumatic drill digging up the road? Of all the varieties of modern pollution, noise is the most insidious.

Yet in the year 1000 the hedgerows actually had a sound. You could hear baby birds chirping in their nests, and the only mechanical noise you would hear came from the wheezing of the blacksmith's bellows. In some villages you might have heard the bell in the church tower, or the creaking and clunking of the wooden cogs in one of the watermills that had been constructed in the last 200 years, and if you lived near one of England's dozen or so cathedrals, you would have heard the heavy metal cascadings of sound from the copper windpipes of one of the recently imported church organs. But that was all. As bees buzzed and wood pigeons cooed, you could listen to God's creation and take pleasure in its subtle variety.

The year 1000 was an empty world, with much more room to stretch out and breathe. With a total English population of little more than a million, there was just one person for every forty or fifty with whom we are surrounded today, and most people lived in small communities, a couple of dozen or so homes circling a village green or extending up and down a single, winding street — the archetypal little village or hamlet to which the modern suburban cul-de-sac pays nostalgic homage. The centuries leading up to 1000 A.D. were the years in which people picked out the crossroads, valley, or stream-crossing where they thought they could piece together a living. Villages built around a green may originally have been constructed in a circular pattern to provide protection for livestock against wolves or other marauders. By the end of the first millennium almost every modern English village existed and bore its modern name, and these names can tell us whether the identity of that village was primarily shaped by the Anglo-Saxons or the Danes.

Place names ending in *ham*, the Old English for "settlement," indicate an Anglo-Saxon origin — as in Durham, Clapham, or Sandringham. Other Anglo-Saxon endings include *ing* (as in Reading), *stowe* (as in Felixstowe), *stead* (as in Hampstead), and *ton* (as in Kingston). Viking settlements can be identified by the ending *by*, which originally meant a farm (as in Whitby, Derby, or Grimsby); and other Danish endings include *thorpe* (as in Scunthorpe), *toft*, meaning a plot of land (as in Lowestoft), and *scale*, meaning a temporary hut or shelter (as in Windscale).

Armed with these pedigrees, we can look at the names of villages along a stretch of marshy Lincolnshire coast to see how the Anglo-Saxons and the Danes rubbed shoulders. The Anglo-Saxons lived inland in settlements like Covenham and Alvingham. But less than five miles away there were Danes living in North Thoresby, or closer to the sea at Grainthorpe. And then there were places where the two heritages mingled. The town of Melton almost certainly started out as the Anglo-Saxon settlement of Middletoun. But when the Vikings came along, they changed Middle to Meddle, and the succeeding years smoothed down Meddletoun to Melton.[28]

The village where he lived was the beginning and almost the end of the Englishman's world. He knew that he lived in Engla-lond, and he probably knew the name of the king whose crude image was stamped on the coins that were starting to play quite a role in the village economy. He would have also made excursions to the tops of the nearest hills to gaze out on other villages which he might have visited, and he had almost certainly made his way to the nearest market town along one of the deep, sunken tracks that wound their way between the fields.

As he stood on the hilltop, he would not have seen significantly more woodland than we would today. It is frequently supposed that medieval England was clad in thick forests, but Neolithic Britons had started cutting down trees and growing crops as early as 5000 B.C., and the Romans were major land managers, laying down villas and farms, as well as their roads, across the countryside. Anglo-Saxon plough teams continued the process, so an Anglo-Saxon standing on the top of, say, Box Hill in Surrey in the year 1000 would have looked out on a pattern of vegetation that was little different from that surveyed by Jane Austen's Emma eight hundred years later.

That Anglo-Saxon would also have seen one or two of the bright, new stone parish churches that were to become the heart of English village life in the second millennium. England's earliest Christian missionaries were monks who went out from the cathedral abbeys to preach at the foot of the tall crosses that survive in the centre of a few ancient towns and villages today. The tall cross marked the point where the people of the village gathered to pray, but as the church grew richer, congregations were able to build themselves houses of worship, first in wood and later in stone.

The Englishman's own home was certainly a wooden structure, based on a framework of sturdy beams stuck into the ground and fastened together with wooden pegs. This framework was then covered in planks or served as the basis for a heavy, basket-like weaving of willow or hazel branches that were covered in "cob" — a mixture of clay, straw, and cow dung that was used until quite recent times for the construction of cottages in Somerset and Devon. Roofs were thatched with straw or reeds, while windows were small gaps cut into the walls and covered with wattle shutters, since glass — the product of beechwood ash fired in a charcoal furnace with washed sand — was a precious, and probably an imported, commodity.[29]

Village communities provided reassuringly constant backdrops for a life. The average Anglo-Saxon could probably recognise every duck, chicken, and pig in his village and knew whom it belonged to — as he knew everything about his neighbours' lives. His social circle would not have filled three or four pages in a modern Filofax, and he would never have needed fresh leaves for updating, since the parents of his neighbours had been his parents' neighbours, and their children were destined to live their lives side-by-side with his. How else could life be? The closest modern parallel is with the restricted and repetitious circle of friends that surround the central families of radio and television soap-opera characters. In the year 1000, the same Christian names were often passed down traditionally inside families, but there were no surnames. There was not yet any need for them.

In the countryside around the villages, the fields were beginning to take on a shape that we would recognise, thanks to the labours of the ploughman with his powerful but cumbersome train of oxen. They cut the soil deep and long, but they were awkward to turn when the end of the furrow had been reached. So just as the village livestock grazed together on communal pasture, the fields created for arable cultivation were also organised on a community basis, with each unit of ploughland taking the form of a long and comparatively narrow strip.

Aelfric, the Cerne Abbas schoolteacher, got his pupils to practice their Latin by learning a dialogue in which the pupils played the parts of different farm labourers, describing their work to a master who cross-questioned them:

Master	What do you say, ploughman? How do you carry out your work?
"Ploughman"	Oh, I work very hard, dear lord. I go out at daybreak driving the oxen to the field, and yoke them to the plough; for fear of my lord, there is no winter so severe that I dare hide at home; but the oxen having been yoked and the share and coulter fastened to the plough, I must plough a full acre or more every day.
Master	Have you any companion?
"Ploughman"	I have a lad driving the oxen with a goad, who is now also hoarse because of the cold and shouting.
Master	What else do you do in the day?
"Ploughman"	I do more than that, certainly. I have to fill

	the oxen's bins with hay, and water them,
	and carry their muck outside.
Master	Oh, oh! It's hard work.
"Ploughman"	It's hard work, sir, because I am not free.

The ploughman's colloquy draws attention to the basic and unromantic reality of English life in the year 1000 — the reliance on slave labour. In 1066 the Normans were to bring to England their military-based arrangement of landholding known to generations of school children as the feudal system, with the hierarchy of serfs, villeins, and lords whose niceties are much argued over by historians. But prior to 1066, virtually all the documentary sources — wills, land deeds, and the literature of the day — clearly show that the basic underpinning of the rural economy in several parts of England was a class of workers who can only be described as slaves.

It is a commonplace that slavery made up the basis of life in the classical world, but it is sometimes assumed that slavery came to an end with the fall of Rome. In fact, the Germanic tribes who conquered Rome captured, kept, and traded in slaves as energetically as the Romans did — as indeed did the Arab conquerors of the Mediterranean. The purpose of war from the fifth to the tenth centuries was as much to capture bodies as it was to capture land, and the tribes of central Germany enjoyed particular success raiding their Slavic neighbours. If you purchased a bondservant in Europe in the centuries leading up to the year 1000, the chances were that he or she was a "Slav" — hence the word "slave."

In England, the Anglo-Saxons proved to be slavers on a par with their Germanic cousins. *Weallas*, or Welshman, was one of the Old English words for slave — which showed where the Anglo-Saxons got their slaves. When, in 1086 A.D., the Normans commissioned their Domesday survey of the land they had conquered, it showed that there were significantly more slaves in the west of England than in the east, reflecting the closeness of Wales, and also the fact that Bristol was a slave port, trading with the Viking merchants based in Ireland. According to contemporary chronicles, eleventh-century Dublin operated the largest slave market in western Europe.

But war was not the only source of slaves. Anglo-Saxon law codes cited "slavery" as the penalty for offences ranging from certain types of theft to incest. In this latter case, the male involved became a slave of the king, while the woman was consigned to the service of the local bishop.[30] Execution was evidently considered too severe a penalty for such an offence, while long-term imprisonment was not a practical possibility. Prisons did not develop until stone buildings and iron bars made them feasible, and since impoverished offenders had no money to pay fines, the only thing they could forfeit was their labour.

People also surrendered themselves into bondage at times of famine or distress, when they simply could not provide for their families any more. In later centuries there was the poorhouse or the bankruptcy law to help cope with such tragedies, but in the year 1000 the starving man had no other resort but to kneel before his lord or lady and place his head in their hands. No legal document was involved, and the new bondsman would be handed a bill-hook or ox-goad in token of his fresh start in servitude. It was a basic transaction — heads for food. The original old English meaning of lord was "loaf-giver," and Geatfleda, a lady of Northumbria, made the transaction explicit in the will she drew up in the 990s: "for the love of God and for the need of her soul, [Geatfleda] has given freedom to Ecceard, the blacksmith, and Aelfstan and his wife and all their off-spring, born and unborn, and Arcil and Cole and Ecgferth [and] Ealdhun's daughter, and all those people whose heads she took for their food in the evil days."[31]

Slavery still exists today in a few corners of the world, and from the security of our own freedom, we find the concept degrading and inhuman. But in the year 1000 very few people were free in the sense that we understand the word today. Almost everyone was beholden to someone more powerful than themselves, and the men and women who had surrendered themselves into bondage lived in conditions that were little different to those of any other member of the labouring classes. "Slave" is the only way to describe their servitude, but we should not envisage them manacled like a galley slave in ancient times, or living in segregated barracks like eighteenth-century slaves on the cotton plantations — or, indeed, like the workers in South African mines in our own times. Most bondsmen lived in what we would now describe as "tied" accommodation in a village with their families, and probably reared their own livestock as well. They were the men with the spades.

In the year 1000 people could not imagine themselves without a protector. You had a lord in heaven and you needed a lord on earth. The ploughman in Aelfric's *Colloquy* talked resentfully about his fear of his lord, and the fact that he worked so hard because his master required it. But other medieval documents proposed faithful service to a good master as a considerable — even a life-fulfilling — source of satisfaction, as it was for many servants right into our own times. It is a late twentieth-century innovation to scorn the concept of "service." In the year 1000 every English village had its local lord who provided an umbrella of protection for his neighbourhood, and that relationship involved a significant element of mutual respect. Anglo-Saxon lords never exercised, or attempted to claim, the notorious *droit de seigneur* whereby manorial law in some parts of Europe gave the local lord the right to bed the young brides of the village on their wedding night, and there were significant limits on their powers.

The great English churchman of the time was Wulfstan of York, the Billy Graham of the year 1000, whose fire-and-brimstone sermons had folk trembling. As chief executive of two major dioceses — Wulfstan was bishop of Worcester as well as archbishop of York — the great orator had to administer one of the largest sets of landholdings in England, and according to one theory he was the author of the *Rectitudines Singularum Personarum*,[32] a tract which tried to set down the rights and obligations that regulated lordship and servitude. In a connected document on the duties of the estate manager, or reeve,[33] the archbishop examined the mechanics of how a successful farm business worked, listing all the spades, shovels, rakes, hoes, ox-goads, buckets, barrels, flails, sieves, and other tools that were needed, right down to the last mousetrap.

Wulfstan described the various types of worker one might find living in the average Anglo-Saxon village, and

his account makes it clear that the ploughman and his assis-
tant with the ox-goad were almost certainly bondsmen,
looking after the team of oxen belonging to the local lord,
who might be a bishop, the head of a monastery, or a nobleman. The ox-team's primary task was to plough the lord's
land, but it also ploughed the strips of the village's other
inhabitants, who paid for this service with various sorts of
rent in kind.

Wulfstan listed the dues and the perks of a centralised
and authoritarian system which allowed space for free enterprise: if the ox-herd had his own cow, he could pasture it
with his lord's oxen; it was the shepherd's perk to retain the
use of twelve nights' dung at Christmas and also to keep the
milk of his flock for the first seven days after the equinox;
the cottager was someone who farmed at least five acres of
land and who paid for this by working for his lord every
Monday in the year, as well as for three days a week in
August as the harvest approached. Nor was just turning up
for a day good enough. The cottager would be expected to
reap a whole acre of oats in the course of one August day, or
half an acre of wheat — though he was allowed to go home
with a sheaf for himself as a bonus.

Wulfstan sketched out the intricacies of give and take on
any estate, emphasising how regulations should be flexible
and responsive to varying local conditions. "One must learn
the laws in a district lovingly," he wrote, "if one does not
wish to lose good opinion on the estate," and he concluded
his survey with a catalogue of the mechanics of celebration
which brought everyone together at the key stages of the
farming year — a harvest feast after reaping, a drinking
feast for ploughing, a reward for successful mowing, a meal

at the haystack, a log from the wagon at wood carrying, a rick-cup at corn carrying, "and many things which I cannot recount."[34]

Unrelenting though they were, the labours of the month involved moments of great fun and celebration in the year 1000, and as March drew to an end, the village looked forward to one of the greatest festivals of all — Easter.

APRIL

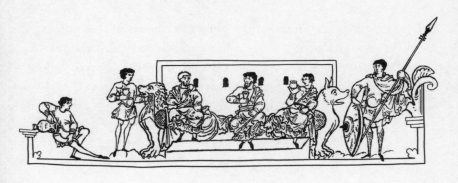

FEASTING

EOSTRE WAS THE GODDESS OF DAWN FOR the tribes of Scandinavia. Her name came from "east," the direction from which the sun arrived every morning, and her special festival was the spring equinox — the dawn of the sun's reign in the northern year. Pagan tradition told of the "Year King," the human victim who was chosen and sacrificed as winter turned into spring. Buried in the fields, his body would come magically to life again with the rising grain, and everyone could share in the miracle of his rebirth by eating the bread that was made from that grain.

The Christian festival of Easter embraced these pre-Christian traditions. Following Bede's calculations, the English Catholic church celebrated Easter on the first Sunday following the first full moon after the spring equinox, and worshippers were encouraged to experience Christ's Passion almost personally. There was a tradition that people should refrain from using nails or iron tools on Good Friday in remembrance of the iron that pierced Christ's hands on Calvary, and next day worshippers went to church for a sombre Saturday ritual of vigil that followed

Christ into the tomb, with five grains of incense being put into a candle to signify the Saviour's five wounds.

In the celebrations of Easter Sunday, the Eucharist took on special significance, since Easter was one of the rare feast days — the others were Christmas and Whitsun — when the ordinary members of the congregation were allowed to consume the bread and wine themselves. This was not a matter of doctrine but of availability. There simply was not that much wine and bread to go round on a weekly basis, and Aelfric took advantage of the specialness of the occasion to explain the significance of the sacrament in a homily that was composed for parish priests to read out in their local churches:

> Dearly beloved, you have frequently been told about our Saviour's resurrection, how on this present day He rose up in strength from death after his Passion. Now, by the grace of God, we will explain to you about the Holy Eucharist to which you must now go . . . lest any doubt concerning the living food might harm you.
>
> . . . Now certain men have often questioned, and still frequently question, how the bread which is prepared from grain and baked by the heat of the fire can be changed into Christ's body; or the wine, which is pressed out from many grapes, becomes changed, by any blessing, into the Lord's blood?
>
> Now we say to such men that some things are said about Christ figuratively. . . . He is called "bread" and "lamb" and "lion" and so forth figuratively. He is called "bread" because he is our life, and the life of the angels; he is called "lamb" on account of his innocence; a "lion"

on account of the strength with which he overcomes
the powerful Devil. But nevertheless according to true
nature, Christ is neither bread, nor lamb, nor lion. . . .

If we consider the Holy Eucharist in a bodily sense,
then we see that . . . it is corruptible bread and corruptible wine, and by the power of the divine word it is truly
Christ's body and his blood; not, however, bodily, but
spiritually.[35]

Aelfric's teaching on the Eucharist differed significantly
from the later doctrine of transubstantiation as fixed by the
Catholic Church. In stressing the symbolism of the bread
and wine, the monk was almost Protestant in his teaching,
and the treatise on which he based his homily was later
condemned and ordered to be destroyed by the Roman
church. But what strikes the modern reader is less the
theology than the clarity and power of the monk's exposi-
tion of a complicated subject, composed and conveyed (in
Englisc) without condescension or oversimplification.

The Easter feast was appreciated the more by people who
had encountered the reality of famine. Today we watch
famine on television, but it is scarcely a source of personal
anxiety to those of us who live in the developed West. It is
another of the crucial distinctions between us and the year
1000, where the possibility of famine was ever-present and
haunted the imagination.

"I shall provide . . . the necessities for life," promised Piers
Plowman in the late medieval fable — with one proviso:
"unless the land fails."[36] Natural disaster and the hardship
that it caused were constant spectres. People dated their
lives by the years when the land and weather failed, and the

pages of the *Anglo-Saxon Chronicle* listed the milestones of misery:

975 Came a very great famine. . . .

976 Here in this year was the great famine in the English race. . . .

986 Here the great pestilence among cattle first came to England. . . .

1005 Here in this year there was the great famine throughout the English race, such that no one ever remembered one so grim before. . . .

1014 In this year on St. Michael's Eve [September 28] that great sea-flood came widely throughout this country, and ran further inland than it ever did before, and drowned many settlements and a countless number of human beings. . . .

1041 All that year was a very heavy time in many and various ways: both in bad weather and crops of the earth; and during this year more cattle died than anyone remembered before, both through various diseases and through bad weather.[37]

These were the evil years when men were compelled to kneel and place their heads in the hands of their lord. In time of famine, according to one Anglo-Saxon law code, "a father may sell his son aged under seven as a slave if necessity forces him to do so,"[38] and even infanticide was not accounted a crime.[39] Bede tells an affecting story of suicide pacts among the seventh-century victims of famine in Sussex: "Frequently forty or fifty emaciated and starving people would go to a cliff, or to the edge of the sea, where they would join hands and leap over, to die by the fall or by drowning."[40] It is not surprising that another chronicle of these years records that "men ate each other."[41]

Cannibalism was only a ghastly folk memory for people living in the year 1000, but everyone knew the reality of scavenging the woods for beechnuts and for the other marginal foodstuffs which, in better times, were left for pigs. Charred acorns have been found in the excavations of Anglo-Saxon settlements, and it is known that acorns, beans, peas, and even bark were ground down to supplement flour when grain stocks grew low. In times of scarcity, people were not ashamed to scour the hedgerows for herbs, roots, nettles, wild grasses — anything to allay the pangs of starvation.

"What makes bitter things sweet?" asked Alcuin, the Yorkshire schoolmaster who went to reform Frankish education for the emperor Charlemagne in the eighth century. "Hunger."

Fasting was the church's way of harnessing hunger to spiritual purposes, and Easter came at the end of the forty-day fast of Lent. Occurring when it did, in the final months of winter when the barns and granaries were getting bare, there was a sense in which Lent made a virtue of necessity. But fasting was a process which elevated material concerns to a higher plain — a means of personal purification and the way to get God on your side. Perhaps choosing a lack would induce God to give plenty. The rhythm of fasting and feasting was another medieval experience which is foreign to most Westerners today, and it brought a special intensity to the joy with which Easter was celebrated, both in church and at the table after the triumphant Easter morning service.

Meat was the principal ingredient of an Anglo-Saxon

feast — large spit-roast joints of beef being considered the best treat. Mutton was not a particular delicacy. Wulfstan's memorandum of estate management described mutton as a food for slaves, and pork seems also to have been considered routine.

The relatively small amounts of fat on all these meats would be viewed by modern nutritionists with quite a kindly eye. Saturated fat, the source of cholesterol with its related contemporary health problems, is a problem of the intensively reared factory-farmed animals of recent years, with their overabundant "scientific" diets and their lack of exercise. All Anglo-Saxon animals were free range, and the Anglo-Saxons would have been shocked at the idea of ploughing land to produce animal feed. Ploughland was for feeding humans. So farm animals were lean and rangey, their meat containing three times as much protein as fat. With modern, intensively reared animals that ratio is often reversed.[42]

Poultry was considered a luxury food, and it was also recognised as a therapeutic diet for invalids, particularly in broth form. Old English recipe and remedy books show that in the year 1000 chicken soup was already renowned for its soothing and restorative powers. As well as chickens, an Anglo-Saxon feast might feature ducks, geese, pigeons, and various forms of game birds — with venison the most highly prized game of all.

Aelfric's schoolroom colloquy is eloquent on the subject of fish, which his "Fisherman" describes himself catching by net, bait, hook, and basket. We are familiar today with lobster and crab baskets, but fishermen in the year 1000 made much use of the brushwood fishing weirs one can still see in the estuary of the river Severn — wide, fixed funnel-shaped networks of basketwork set out like so many pigeonholes into which fish are swept, then left marooned. Archbishop Wulfstan described the construction of fish weirs as one of the tasks for the summer on the well-run estate, and there were evidently so many of the contraptions in eleventh-century England that they came to hinder river navigation. An enactment in the reign of King Edward the Confessor in the 1060s ordered the destruction of the "fisheries" that hindered the flow of the rivers Thames, Trent, Severn, and Yorkshire Ouse.[43]

"Which fish do you catch?" asked the Master in Aelfric's schoolroom dialogue. "Eels and pike, minnows and burbot, trout and lampreys," replied the pupil playing the role of Fisherman.

For modern tastes, this list contains a disconcerting proportion of wriggly and eel-like creatures. The burbot, also called the eel-pout, was a flat-headed fish with two small beards on the nose and one on the chin, while the lamprey was even uglier, sometimes described as a water snake and featuring a large sucker-like mouth with which it attached itself parasitically to other fish. Rich and oily like all eels, lampreys were considered a particular delicacy in the Middle Ages, and famously ended the life of King Henry I, William the Conqueror's youngest son, who was chronicled as dying in 1135 of "a surfeit of lampreys."

Aelfric's fisherman was a talkative and candid character:

Master	Why don't you fish in the sea?
"Fisherman"	Sometimes I do, but rarely, because it is a lot of rowing for me to the sea.

Master	What do you catch in the sea?
"Fisherman"	Herrings and salmon, porpoises and sturgeon, oysters and crabs, mussels, winkles, cockles, plaice and flounders and lobsters, and many similar things.
Master	Would you like to catch a whale?
"Fisherman"	Not me!
Master	Why?
"Fisherman"	Because it is a risky business catching a whale. It's safer for me to go on the river with my boat, than to go hunting whales with many boats.
Master	Why so?
"Fisherman"	Because I prefer to catch a fish that I can kill, rather than a fish that can sink or kill not only me but also my companions with a single blow.
Master	Nevertheless, many do catch whales and escape danger, and make a great profit by it.
"Fisherman"	You are right, but I dare not because of my timid spirit!

Aelfric had evidently heard of fishermen ganging together in hunting packs of small open boats, as they still do in the Faroe Islands, to corner a whale in an inlet, then drive it ashore. *Craspois*, salt whale blubber, was imported to London around the year 1000, and some nutritionists have wondered if this reflected a physiological need. Anglo-Saxon dwellings were so poorly heated, runs this theory, that the diet of the time had to provide an extra-thick layer of body insulation.

Feasting, however, was about much more than mere nutrition, since conviviality lay at the very heart of Anglo-

Saxon life. The memorandum of estate management attributed to Wulfstan depicted the seasonal celebrations as moments for which the community lived, and the archbishop himself was famous for his lavish hospitality, even as he personally observed the rules of clerical restraint. Abstaining as a pious monk from both alcohol and meat, he nevertheless provided his guests with generous quantities of both, sitting in their midst while consuming his own meagre fare. His personal inclinations made him the vegetarian in the corner, but his role as archbishop and prince of the church made it important that he should also demonstrate hospitality and act as the lord of the feast.

The epic poems of the time all come to rest in banqueting halls. Who is not familiar with the classic medieval scene of lord and lady gathered with their retainers in a great wooden hall like an old tithe barn? There are beams and rafters and draughts through the walls, with a fire in the middle of the floor and damp rising up through the greasy floor covering of rushes, into which have been flung the old chicken bones. It is a tableau much caricatured in modern costume dramas, but archaeological excavations confirm most of the physical details, right down to the blow-fly maggots germinating among the refuse on the floor.

"The warriors laughed, there was a hum of contentment," runs *Beowulf*'s description of an Anglo-Saxon feast, and we catch that same atmosphere from the April drawing in the Julius Work Calendar, with the revellers seated side by side on what the heroic poems call the *medu-benc* — the mead bench. In the year 1000 a noble feast was a lavishly staged affair, and the wills of the period suggest that people's most prized possessions were the accoutrements with which they entertained. Reading the inventories, you can imagine yourself at the dinner party — hall tapestries and seat covers, "a table cover with all the cloths that go with it,"[44] candlesticks, and elaborate drinking vessels which must have resembled the drinking horn being filled by the young lad on the left of this month's calendar drawing. Archaeological excavations have uncovered some particularly large and beautiful drinking horns, along with ceremonial jewellery and ornamented goblets — but no cutlery. The eating fork was not invented until the seventeenth century, and when you went to a feast you took your own knife.

Mead was the reveller's drink of choice, according to the sagas. It was a supersweet, alcoholic beverage with quite a kick, brewed from the crushed refuse of honeycombs.[45] Less common was wine — which was also less alcoholic. The yeasts on English grapes rarely produced more than 4 percent alcohol, and there were no hermetically corked glass bottles in which the drink could acquire a laid-down "vintage" character, since the corked wine bottle was not developed until the eighteenth century. Anglo-Saxon wine was kept in wooden barrels and leather flasks.

"I am a binder and a scourger and soon become a thrower," ran a riddle of the time, inviting puzzlers to guess the identity of an alcoholic beverage. "Sometimes I cast an old fellow right to the ground."[46]

The answer was mead, not wine, for most Anglo-Saxon wine was light and fruity, rather like Beaujolais nouveau today, consumed soon after the harvest, and only intended to last until the next harvest came round.

Nor was *beor* strong enough to produce intense intoxication. Hops were grown in the year 1000, but they were used only in cloth-dyeing processes. Not until the fourteenth century is there evidence of hops being generally used to give English beer its bitterness — as well as a longer shelf life. Like wine, the ale of the year 1000 had to be consumed without delay, and it was probably quite a sweet beverage with a porridgy consistency.

Ale was the drink of the Middle Ages, much safer to consume than water, since its boiling and brewing provided some sort of protection against contamination. The solid texture of all Anglo-Saxon beverages was reflected by a utensil that is used today only in the kitchen — the sieve — which is found in the early Anglo-Saxon graves of high-born women in the form of decorative sieve-spoons. These elaborate and precious implements were signs of status, possibly worn round the neck as a sommelier wears his wine saucer today, since it was the ceremonial duty of high-born women to serve the drinks at their menfolk's feasts:

> *Wealhtheow came forward* [relates *Beowulf*],
> *Mindful of ceremonial — she was Hrothgar's queen.*
> *Adorned with gold, that proud woman*
> *Greeted the men in the hall, then offered the cup*
> *To the Danish king first of all.*[47]

The ceremonial feast was the setting in which the Anglo-Saxon monarch displayed his power and dignity. The royal court was something like a circus, touring an annual round of locations in which it successively satisfied then exhausted its welcome. The Easter gathering was one of the principal courts of the year. We can imagine the coming and going of fifty to two hundred people, arriving with their horses that had to be fed and watered, along with the petitioners, favour seekers, and great of the land invited to join the king in worship, do business, reaffirm loyalty, and feast in the time-honoured fashion.

The great kingdoms and empires of these years were built around the personalities of charismatic leaders like Alfred and Charlemagne, and the maintenance of power depended on itinerant pressings of the flesh. In the year 1000 the king of England was Alfred's great-great-grandson, Ethelred — nicknamed "Ethelred Unred" by unkind chroniclers after his death. "Unred" was mistranslated in later years as "Unready," and Ethelred has been known to history as "the Unready" ever since.

In fact, "Unred" meant "ill-advised" in Old English. It was a rhyming pun on the *Englisc* meaning of Ethelred's name: "of noble counsel." He was "the well-advised, ill-advised" — "of noble counsel, rubbish counsel" — and that paradox summed up the character of his lengthy reign. In the year 1000, Ethelred had already been on the throne for twenty-two years, and life as one of his subjects had been a complicated and contradictory experience: the best of times in some ways, but the worst of times as well.

MAY

WEALTH AND WOOL

I F KING ETHELRED UNRED — ETHELRED THE
Unready — had died in or around the year 1000, he
might have had a reputation to match that of his distinguished forebear Athelstan, the first king of all Engla-lond.
After 1000 A.D. Ethelred was to struggle with a succession
of problems which eventually drove him into exile and an
ignominious death. But viewed from the year 1000, it was
arguable that he had brought England's first millennium to
a laudable close. The kingdom was more unified and richer
than ever. In 1000 A.D., in fact, England enjoyed a prosperity and civilisation unmatched in northern Europe.

The evidence is in the coins. They are found almost
everywhere that late Anglo-Saxon remains are excavated.
Thin and smooth, they are elegant little wafers of ham-
mered high-grade silver which nestle cosily in the palm.
They are duller and lighter than modern machine-made
coins, but they are bursting with personality — and also
with clues to the complex getting and spending which they
sustained.

The image of Ethelred himself is marked with the same
ambivalence that characterised his reign. On one coin,

which depicts the hand of Providence reaching down dramatically out of the clouds, the king looks wise and saintly, something like a bishop. He has a ceremonial cope pulled around his neck. But on another, on which he is shown wearing a fiercely spiked military helmet, Ethelred looks like a crazed version of Alexander the Great. He wears a cockatoo headdress and seems raring to take on the world. Both images are essentially symbolic, intended to convey the idea of kingship, rather than a photographic reproduction of Ethelred's face, and they may reflect the varied messages that Ethelred was trying to convey at different times as he struggled to cope with the shifting challenges of his reign.

It is the letters on the coin around the face which tell us more — though unlike modern coins, they state no date. (The earliest known date on any European coin is 1234 A.D.) Instead, the coded hieroglyphics tell us who minted the coin and where, and from this data we can reconstruct the framework of a remarkably sophisticated economic and administrative system that reached from one end of England to the other.

England's coinage was the most advanced in western Europe in the year 1000, with a network of over seventy local mints spread around the country, each of them inside a market town, or within a dozen or so miles of one. This made it possible for money to be carried safely to and from the mint within the hours of daylight. The mints were probably protected by stockades, and each was directed by a "moneyer" who was in charge of the coin-making process.

By the reign of King Ethelred at the end of the tenth century, English coins were issued for limited periods of validity — no more than two or three years. At the end of that period the coins ceased to be legal tender, and to redeem their value you had to take them to your local mint where, for every ten you returned, you received eight or nine of the new issue. The difference between what you gave and what you received constituted a government tax, and that made the "moneyer" effectively the king's tax collector.

People accepted this system because it guaranteed good and trustworthy coins. The soft silver alloys of the time were easy to shave or clip, so regular issues of fresh-minted coins made counterfeiting more difficult. The English silver penny, the standard English unit of currency in the year 1000, was not pure silver, but it contained a high and constant proportion of silver in its alloy — about 92.5 percent — and Anglo-Saxon kings kept that proportion constant.

The local moneyer was probably a full-time government official in busy mints like London, Winchester, and Canterbury, where there was a heavy inflow of foreign coins to be melted down and reminted. In the more distant, provincial mints, the moneyer may well have been the local jeweller or goldsmith, who produced coins under licence from the king. Harsh penalties were laid down for issuing coins that were basely alloyed or too light: "If a moneyer is found guilty [of issuing base or light coins]," read Clause 14 of Athelstan's Second Code of Laws, "the hand shall be cut off with which he committed the crime, and fastened up on the mint."[48]

Each moneyer had his own licensed die, or coin stamp, with which he would imprint every coin with his personal details. We can imagine the die mounted on a wooden stand, beside the bench on which the moneyer beat out the sheets of silver alloy to the correct thickness and ratio of precious metal to alloy. He then cut this sheet of metal into identical small squares, each of them a coin blank slightly larger than the circumference of the die on his bench. To produce one penny, the moneyer would place a blank onto the die, and would strike the blank smartly downwards with a mallet. This drove the blank into the die, imprinting the lower surface of the coin with the moneyer's mark and local details.

To complete the making of the coin, the moneyer would then place the official die that was engraved with the royal head and the distinguishing particulars of the new issue on top of the blank and strike downwards for a second time. When the edges had been trimmed, the result was one silver penny, and if people wanted a half-penny, then they cut it across the middle. In the year 1000 a half-penny was exactly that — a half-circle of dull silver alloy.

England's seventy or so mints hand-produced five to ten million coins every two to three years by this meticulous and controlled process, an enormous quantity of bullion unmatched by any other country in Europe. Some of the silver came from England itself. There were small silver workings in Derbyshire, Gloucestershire, Devon, and the Mendip Hills in Somerset. But modern chemical analysis of the many hoards that have been excavated shows that the ore was, for the most part, mined in Germany, where rich silver deposits had recently been discovered in the Harz mountains. This indicates that silver bullion was flowing into England in large quantities in the years leading up to 1000 A.D. — a very healthy balance of trade. But what was

England selling to the outside world to generate such a positive cash flow?

Here we venture into territory where the scarcity of evidence calls for historical detective work, since documentary sources on life and events in the years around 1000 are tragically sparse — in singular contrast to our own day, where the most trivial corners of life generate mountains of data every day. The modern chronicler of, say, sexual behaviour at the end of the second millennium already has thirty-six cartons of documents to cover the high jinks of the President of the United States alone — which is thirty or more than the storage space occupied by the modern transcripts of *everything* surviving in *Englisc*.

The historian who would examine such a private subject as sexual behaviour in the years around 1000 has virtually nothing to work with beyond a group of sentences in the *Life of St. Dunstan*, describing the decadent King Eadwig, who scandalised the great of the land by failing to appear at his coronation feast in 955 A.D. When Dunstan dared to enter the royal bedchamber, he found the jewelled crown of England disrespectfully thrown on the floor, and the king energetically enjoying the charms of a young lady who, for all we know, could well have been the Anglo-Saxon equivalent of a White House intern — with her mother cavorting in the same bed beside her.[49]

It was the Normans who first set about obliterating evidence of the robust native culture that existed in England before their arrival in 1066. Every Anglo-Saxon cathedral was almost totally rebuilt. But it was the chaos that followed Henry VIII's dissolution of the monasteries in the sixteenth century which led to the worst destruction of all.

Priceless ancient manuscripts were burned, used as drum-skins and roof insulation, or to line beer barrels and bind books.[50] As a consequence, it only takes a morning to read all surviving Anglo-Saxon poetry — and of England's principal commerce at the turn of the first millennium we know even less than we do about King Eadwig's sex life.

Two hundred years after 1000 A.D. England was clearly established as the principal supplier of high-quality wool to northern Europe. By the twelfth and thirteenth centuries, the Cotswold villages and towns, the South Downs and saltmarshes, the lowlands of East Anglia, and the slopes of the Yorkshire Pennines were all prosperous areas thronged with sheep. They were the basis of a flourishing industry that exported wool to the great cloth factories of Flanders, and subsequent documentary evidence demonstrates how wool was the source of England's wealth — the backbone of its economy and culture. When the Lord Chancellor started presiding over the House of Lords, he sat on a wool-sack. Journeymen travelled to the local markets to buy up the produce of England's many thousands of prosperous sheep farmers, and a network of packhorses and muletrains systematically transported the wool in convoys to the ports of southeast England, where merchants organised prof-itable flotillas to ferry the wool bales across to the Low Countries.

But we can only deduce that all this existed — or was starting to exist — in the year 1000, for while documents survive that testify to tenth-century trade in wine, furs, fish, and slaves, there is no similar paperwork that shows England exporting wool or woolen cloth. The evidence is indirect, like the legacy of place names — the Isle of Sheppey, for example, and towns like Shipton and Shipley whose names suggest a livelihood derived from sheep. Anglo-Saxon wills regularly discuss the disposition of sheep by the hundred, and excavations reveal sheep bones, sheep shears, wool spindles, weaving batons, and all the paraphernalia of cloth production.

The Anglo-Saxons were clearly sheep-rearing folk, and our calendar drawing for this month reflects that — a flock of delightfully frisky and wool-covered sheep cavorting under the eye of equally contented shepherds. May was the month of shearing, when the animals were first washed and the sheared wool then rinsed in a series of baths. Where necessary, it was lightly greased with butter or lard to facilitate the separation of the individual wool fibres with the heads of thistles or teazles that were used like combs. Then the spinning could commence.[51] The spinning wheel did not appear in Europe until the thirteenth century, but the hand spindles and loom components regularly unearthed from Anglo-Saxon excavations suggest that wool-making must have been a common household process.

The best evidence of commerce is a letter of 796 A.D. from the emperor Charlemagne to Offa, the great king of Mercia, complaining at variations in the size of the *saga*, the woollen cloaks and blankets that Mercia exported to France. Charlemagne asked the king to make sure that the cloths would in future be made to the same size that they used to be.[52] This would seem satisfactory evidence of English woolen cloth being exported to Europe a couple of centuries before the millennium, and from the centuries after 1000 A.D. we know that Norwich, Ipswich, Colchester, Rochester, Dover, and all the principal ports of the southeast were busily involved in the wool trade. Since it is certain that all these ports were healthily in business by the year 1000 exporting *something*, and since we also know that every Viking longship routinely carried a small quantity of rough woven cloth to trade with, it does not seem unreasonable to suppose that ships from the sheep-rich country of Engla-lond engaged in the same trade.

Following in the tradition of predecessors like Athelstan, Ethelred laboured to integrate the prosperous realm he had inherited. The division of England into shires was the most enduring royal achievement of the tenth and eleventh centuries. As the pattern of the country's towns and villages took shape, so England's kings had created administrative units around them — Wiltshire around the town of Wilton, Somerset around Somerton, Hampshire around Hamwic, the modern Southampton, and so on. Staffordshire, Bedfordshire, and Warwickshire were all county units created in the tenth century. In every shire there was a shire court, which administered the king's law, and it was in the reign of Ethelred that the shire reeve, or sheriff, first came into view as the chief executive officer of local government. In a law code issued in 997 A.D. Ethelred ordered the shire reeve and the twelve leading magnates in each locality to swear to accuse no innocent man, nor conceal any guilty one — the earliest English reference to the sworn jury of presentment, ancestor of the Grand Jury which existed in England until 1933, and which still plays a prominent role in the legal processes of the United States of America.[53]

Trade, law, administration — Ethelred displayed considerable skill and application at the arts of peace. But it was his misfortune to be king of a rich and easygoing country at a time when yet another wave of Viking bandits was coming out of the east. Viking is a word of uncertain origin, meaning sea robber according to some authorities, and sea trader according to others. Both meanings apply. The successive Viking waves of raiding out of Scandinavia in the eighth, ninth, and tenth centuries reflected scarcity and disorder at home, while the extraordinary technology of their light and warlike longships enabled them to raid and trade wherever they went.

And the Vikings went everywhere. By the year 1000 they had made themselves the first princes of Russia and Kiev. They raided Spain, and provided the mercenaries who made up the Varangian guard for the Byzantine emperors in Constantinople. In the tenth century, they took over part of northern France, turning themselves from Norsemen into Normans and securing French recognition of the duchy of Normandy. They were the inhabitants of England's Danelaw. The raiders who started harassing the south and west coasts of Ethelred's kingdom in the early 980s were following in the footsteps of the invaders against whom Alfred had fought only a hundred years earlier. In 988 a major fleet of longships sailed up the Bristol Channel, landed men at Watchet, and raided arrogantly down through Somerset into Devon.

The Vikings were the fresher and better organised for being able to anchor their ships in the ports of Normandy, where their kinsfolk now spoke French and practised Christianity. When the Pope reproached Duke Richard of Normandy in the early 990s for providing such comfort to the enemies of his English neighbours, Richard agreed to stop giving shelter to longships destined for England. A treaty was signed between Ethelred and Richard, binding each side not to entertain the other's enemies — the first step in a relationship between England and Normandy that would have huge consequences for both countries. But there was no evidence of the Normans working hard to give effect to the agreement, and over on the northern side of the Channel, the Vikings kept coming.

In the summer of 991 a fleet of ninety-three longships sailed into the Thames estuary and ravaged the ports and villages on the coasts of East Anglia and Kent. Most communities paid large ransoms to be rid of the raiders, but the men of Essex rallied outside the port of Maldon under the leadership of their proud, white-haired leader, Byrhtnoth. The Vikings had landed on an island connected to the mainland by a causeway that was visible only at low tide, and the English could have picked the raiders off as they tried to make the mainland. But the overconfident Byrhtnoth honorably agreed to a Viking request that the visitors might be allowed ashore to line up properly before the fight commenced — and the English lost, with terrible slaughter, the earliest recorded example of English fair play on the battlefield.

It was the first entry in the ledger that includes such gentlemanly blunders as the Charge of the Light Brigade, and Byrhtnoth's fruitless valour was promptly commemorated in similarly heroic verse. "The Battle of Maldon" was the "Top of the Pops" of the year 1000, a melancholy but stirring hit-of-the-moment that was sung by poets and recited at mead benches in long winter evenings, and it made a folk hero of the old general who "shook the slim ash-spear" at the Viking foe:

> Though I am white with winters, I will not away,
> For I think to lodge me alongside my dear one,
> Lay me down by my lord's right hand . . .
> English silver is not so softly won.[54]

England's eagerness to mythologise a loser reflected the sad lack of any homegrown winners in the tricky business of fighting off the Vikings in the final years of the first millennium. The raids became a national trauma, particularly for people living near the coast. Every summer brought the prospect of the dragonships snaking their way upriver, each vessel filled with thirty or more rapacious thugs.

Archaeological remains show no evidence of the Vikings wearing their fearsome horned helmets, which seem to be the imaginings of subsequent generations, but the swords, spears, and battle-axes that have been excavated are ferocious and well-crafted weapons. The Vikings were clearly masters of the latest techniques of metal forging, and their tactics were as bloodthirsty as legend. They were after gold, silver, and easily moveable booty, but they were also in search of slaves. Fit young men and nubile young women commanded the highest prices in the slave market at Dublin, and the raiders were ruthless in massacring those who had no saleable value — the old or very young.

"And for long now the English have been entirely without victory," bemoaned Archbishop Wulfstan, "and too much cowed because of the wrath of God, and the pirates are so strong with God's consent, that in battle one will often put flight to ten. . . . And often ten or twelve, one after another, will disgracefully insult the thane's wife, and sometimes his near kinswoman, while he who considered himself proud and powerful and brave enough before that happened, looks on."[55]

King Ethelred's solution to this debilitating challenge was to try to buy the raiders off, either paying them what was effectively protection money to go away or, in some cases, hiring bands of raiders as mercenaries to serve as defenders against their fellows. These payments became popularly known as "Danegeld," and many of the English coins bearing Ethelred's image that have been unearthed by modern archaeologists have been found in Denmark, Norway, and Sweden, where the raiders took their protection money and dug a hole to "put it in the bank."

Ethelred had solid precedent for his policy. In 876 Alfred had paid the Danes to leave Wessex. But whereas Alfred used the time that he bought to get his defences organised, Ethelred lacked the grit and military ability of his famous forefather. Following the Battle of Maldon, he agreed to pay the Vikings twenty thousand pounds in silver and gold, and the raiders duly departed. But they kept returning in the years that followed, ravaging and plundering for months on end before extorting fresh tribute — and Ethelred proved unable to defeat them in battle.

The author of this section of the *Anglo-Saxon Chronicle* made little effort to hide his disgust at his monarch's military incompetence: "When they were in the east, the English army was kept in the west, and when they were in the south, our army was in the north." The king summoned his advisers to work out fresh tactics, "but if anything was then decided, it did not last even a month. Finally there was no leader who would collect an army, but each fled as best he could, and in the end no shire would even help the next."[56]

Ethelred's problems were compounded by the fact that the raiders were in pursuit of more than casual booty. From 994 onwards some of the most effective war parties were led by Sweyn Forkbeard, the king of Denmark, who had territorial ambitions. In one sense, Ethelred's payments of Danegeld were signs of weakness, and they have certainly been treated as such by most historians, starting with the derisive scribes of the *Anglo-Saxon Chronicle*. But the ability of England's king to raise large sums of money on a regular basis spoke to a prosperous country and an efficient government machine whose value the king of Denmark could well appreciate.

From 994 to 1000, and then on for another dozen years, Sweyn's forces kept returning to England in ever better organised expeditions. His goal was now total conquest, and as the inhabitants of the old Danelaw observed the contrast in style between Ethelred Unred and the decisive Viking king with his war fleets, loyalties in Essex, East Anglia, and the northeast started to shift in his favour. In modern terms, the annual raids of the dragonships appearing from nowhere, whisking off booty and then vanishing back over the horizon, were like the touchings down of so many alien spaceships, virtually unpredictable and impossible to prevent.

Ethelred tried every angle. In 1002 he concluded a diplomatic marriage with Emma, sister of the duke of Normandy, in an attempt to secure more practical Norman support. He called for a national fast to beseech divine intervention, and in 1008 he gathered the largest navy that

England had ever raised, only to see it turn against itself and disperse in mutiny. In a domestic offensive, he married off two daughters by his first marriage to magnates in Northumbria and East Anglia, hoping to check the growing support that Sweyn of Denmark was commanding there.

It was all in vain. In the summer of 1013 Sweyn disembarked at Gainsborough in Lindsey, twenty miles from the mouth of the Trent, and the whole of Danish England immediately accepted him as king. As Sweyn marched south, Oxford and Winchester surrendered as soon as he appeared. When the magnates of the west gave him their allegiance, the citizens of London, the only centre of resistance, surrendered. The alien leader was installed in power, and Ethelred withdrew into exile in Normandy.

King Sweyn I of England did not have long to enjoy his triumph. He died early in 1014. But his son Canute succeeded him, and though Sweyn's death provoked some revival of Ethelred's fortunes, the unhappy Unred died in 1016, followed by his son Edmund later that year. The young Canute became the undisputed King of England, and he proved a firm and effective ruler. If the famous legend of how the new monarch had his throne placed in the path of the advancing tide is true, it seems likely that Canute staged the event *not* to get the waves to halt in homage to his kingly power, but to prove the very opposite: that there are practical limits to the extent of earthly authority.

Canute died in 1035, and thirty-one years later, in the year that everyone remembers, England was definitively invaded by William the Conqueror and the descendants of the

Scandinavian raiders who had settled in Normandy. The invasion of 1066 is generally thought of as French, and that was certainly true in linguistic terms. But its roots and self-image went back to the Vikings. So while the years around 1000 saw a flowering of Anglo-Saxon civilisation, they were also scarred by the crude and naked force that would bring that flowering to an end.

JUNE

LIFE IN TOWN

PLOUGHLAND, PASTURE, AND WOODLAND — in the year 1000 the forests were farmed like fields. Wood was the fuel of the times, and it was also the principal building material, the substance of choice for every sort of household implement and repair. Technically the first millennium fell in the Iron Age, but when it came to the texture of everyday life it was much more the Age of Wood.

"Which of you doesn't make use of my craft, when I make houses and various vessels and boats for you all?" asked the carpenter boastfully in Aelfric's *Colloquy*.[57]

The word *carpenter* is said to have come from the admiration which the Romans felt for the fine and sturdy two-wheeled cart developed by the Celtic woodworkers of ancient Britain — not dissimilar to the cart depicted in this month's calendar drawing. The Romans called it a "carpentum," and those who were skilled at making such carts — or who used the wood transported in them — became known as carpenters.[58]

People ate off wood. Anglo-Saxon excavations show many more wooden platters than earthenware plates. People drank from ash or alderwood cups that were turned on a foot-pedalled pole lathe. A leather thong was tied to a pole above the carpenter's head, wrapped around the lathe, then run down to the foot pedal. By keeping the thong tight around the lathe and by pedalling hard, the carpenter could get his piece of wood turning in alternately clockwise and counterclockwise directions — a simple but effective piece of self-powered technology that was still in use in English woodworking shops on the eve of the Second World War.

The forest was the mysterious home where the ancient spirits of the woodland lived. People foraged for firewood there. Its leaves provided winter bedding for cattle. Its charcoal pits supplied high-intensity fuel for the blacksmith. The forest was a place of refuge when the Vikings came, and in time of famine it was the larder of last resort. But most of all, in the year 1000, the farmed coppices of England's woodlands provided timber for the increasing numbers of towns being built all over the country.

The Romans based their occupation of Britain around a few fortified and elegant urban communities, which were resorts and garrisons as much as they were towns. Living in a city, or *civitus*, was the essence of Roman civilisation, and the barbarians who subdued Rome were literally "uncivilised" in that they were not city dwellers. The Anglo-Saxons only took over a few Roman sites like London, Bath, Cirencester, and Lincoln. Their preferred unit of habitation was the village, and England remained predominantly rural until the reign of King Alfred, when the threat of the Vikings provoked his construction of a network of defended settlements known as *burhs* — the root word of the modern borough.

The classic definition of an Anglo-Saxon town was that it had a defensive wall or stockade, a mint, and a marketplace. Some of Alfred's *burhs* were old settlements refortified. Others were new forts set up in locations which later developed into fully fledged towns. An example of this was the town of Oxford, which was of no special importance in Alfred's reign, to judge from contemporary evidence, but which had developed apace by the year 1000. The tenth-century records of the abbey of Abingdon describe how the citizens of Oxford got together to pay for canal and rechannelling work on the River Thames, so that boats could sail up the river more easily to do business with the town.

Money, and the increasing amount of reliable coinage in circulation, provided the crucial factor in the growth of those towns which developed from Alfred's military centres into marketplaces. Warwick, Stafford, Buckingham, Oxford — most of the county towns of modern England originated in the tenth century. Roughly 10 percent of England's population was living in towns by the year 1000, which meant that the country's farming methods had developed the efficiency to produce a 10 percent surplus — while the town dwellers were generating sufficient profit to purchase the foodstuffs and other supplies they needed.

Eyeing this growth in the money economy with both apprehension and covetousness, Alfred's successors tried to stake their claim to some regulation — and to taking a cut — of the growing volume of urban business:

> I, King Athelstan [ran a decree of around 930 A.D.], with the advice of my Archbishop, Wulfhelm, and my other bishops also, inform the reeve in every borough,

and pray you in the name of God and All His saints, and command you also by my friendship . . . that no one shall buy goods worth more than twenty pence outside a town; but he shall buy within the town, in the presence of the market-reeve or some other trustworthy man, or again, in the presence of the reeve at a public meeting.[59]

This regulation suggests there was a flourishing black economy in Anglo-Saxon England, with businessmen quietly doing deals between themselves, out of sight of the king's reeve and out of reach of his tolls and taxes — and the disappearance of these laws in subsequent generations suggests that the royal attempts to play trade commissar were abandoned. Free enterprise triumphed, and business expanded accordingly. In 1000 A.D. England's chief salt town was Droitwich, near Worcester, where the profusion of natural brine springs was exploited by the locals in a profitable complex of saltpans and furnaces. Anglo-Saxon wills show that landowners as far away as Oxfordshire and Buckinghamshire were making investments in the salt-making plants of Droitwich, while the records of churches in Westminster, Coventry, and even Paris show Droitwich saltpans and furnaces included in their investment portfolios.[60]

Documents from the town of Winchester in these years show how outside investment was starting to push up urban land values. In 975 the clerics of the Old Minster relinquished a large country estate which was yielding them good food-rents in order to obtain a plot of only two acres inside the city, while tenth-century wills and charters from other parts of the country describe the bishop of Chester owning fourteen houses in the town of Stafford, and the abbess of Barking owning no less than twenty-eight in London. Down in the west country a certain Elfgar of the manor of Bishopsworth outside Bristol owned ten houses in the nearby city. On the assumption that these multiple investments in house property had rental and resale implications, we can conclude that England already had its first property developers.[61]

It also had town planners. Alfred's *burhs* were laid out to very regular grids, often arranged as a square, with a regular distance between the streets. Their designers obviously knew about surveying — as is clear from one document which takes us into Winchester on market day. The cattle were herded in the main street and into nearby Gar street, where modern excavations have uncovered the remains of pens, hurdles, and manure of sheep and cattle. The animals passed on to Fleshmonger street, later known as Parchment street, where they were butchered by the tradesmen who lived and worked on the same premises. Nearby was Tanner street, where the cattle's hides were processed into leather, and also Shieldmaker Street, where craftsmen fashioned the tanned leather onto wickerwork or round wooden boards.

We can imagine this busy chain of business working its way through the commercial part of the town, while over at the cathedral the pilgrims arrived by the hundred to venerate the relics of St. Swithin. The town records show a hosier, a shoemaker, and a soapmaker in position to sell their wares to the visitors, along with two meeting halls where the prosperous citizens gathered to feast and drink — early evidence of the civic banquet.[62] These Winchester burghers seem to have been a jolly bunch. The development of town life was to hasten the development of family surnames, which, like street names, were often based on trades and occupations — Tanner, Weaver, Carpenter, and so on. But, in the meantime, Winchester's cheery inhabitants identified each other with affectionate or derisive nicknames: Clean-hand, Fresh-friend, Soft-bread, Foul-beard, Money-taker, Penny-purse, and Penny-feather.[63]

Trade was the life of the town, and by the year 1000 England's merchants had been trading for some time in goods that came from exotic and faraway places. As the Venerable Bede lay dying in 735 A.D., he had called for the "treasures" that he wished to distribute to his fellow monks, and first out of his treasure chest came pepper[64] — which, growing in the East Indies, had travelled tens of thousands of miles by mule train and ship to reach Baghdad and the Mediterranean. It was probably in the northern Italian town of Pavia, the ancient capital of Lombardy, that English merchants had picked up Bede's pepper. Pavia was the great centre of commercial exchange between northwestern Europe and the East, and accounts of the time vividly describe merchants' tents being pitched in the fields beside the river Ticino on the outskirts of the city. Prominent among the merchants were the *gens Anglicorum et Saxorum*, who haggled over silks, spices, ivory, goldwork, and precious stones with merchants from Venice and the southern Italian ports of Amalfi and Salerno.[65]

It had been a tough journey for the Englishmen, down through the Rhineland and over the Alpine passes, and it was small wonder they were in a bad temper when they got there. According to one early eleventh-century document, the English had taken offence at the opening of their bags and baggages by the Pavian customs officials, and had grown violent. The kings of Lombardy and England subsequently held discussions about this outbreak of English hooliganism abroad, and it was agreed that England's merchants could have the right to trade in Pavia free of tolls and transaction taxes, provided that they paid a collective levy every three years.

It is the earliest detailed example of a commercial treaty in English history, and under its terms the English purchased their licence to trade with the triennial payment of fifty pounds of pure silver, two fine greyhounds with gilded and embossed collars, two shields, two swords, and two lances. In an additional clause that was presumably intended to reduce the incentive for local extortion or bribery, provision was made for the Pavian official in charge of the market to receive two fur coats and two pounds of silver as his own cut on the deal.

It was important to stay on the right side of the customs man. A few years earlier, Bishop Liudprand of Cremona, a Lombard envoy, had been stopped by Greek customs officials on his way back to Italy when they opened his bags and discovered that he was carrying bolts of the famous purple silk of Byzantium, the ultimate in prestigious apparel. Liudprand complained that he had brought home purple silk before, but got nowhere: "That," he was told, "was in the time of a negligent ruler." Liudprand then claimed that the Byzantine emperor himself had given him special permission. "The emperor," said the customs man, "must have meant something different. These things are forbidden. . . . This distinction of dress should belong to those alone who surpass other nations in wealth and wisdom."

Liudprand could not contain himself. "In Italy," he retorted, "our lowest prostitutes and fortune tellers wear this colour," and he reported the whole incident to his master:

> So, you see, they judge . . . all other nations unworthy to go about clothed in this way. Is it not indecent and insulting that these soft, effeminate, long-sleeved, bejewelled and begowned liars, eunuchs and idlers should go about in purple, while our heroes, strong men trained to war, full of faith and charity, servants of God, filled with all virtues, may not! If this is not an insult, what is?[66]

Aelfric's "Merchant" had evidently found a way of getting round such problems. Asked about the goods that he was in the habit of bringing to England, he headed his list with "purple cloth and purple silks," followed by "precious jewels and gold, unusual clothes and spices, wine and oil, ivory and bronze, copper and tin, sulphur and glass, and many similar things."

"Do you want to sell your goods here," asked the Master, "for just what you paid for them there?"

"I don't want to," replied the Merchant, displaying an unapologetic profit motive. "What would my labour benefit me then? I want to sell dearer here than I buy there so that I gain some profit, with which I may feed myself and my wife and my sons. . . . I board my ship with my cargo and sail to lands overseas, and sell my goods, and buy precious things which aren't produced in this country. And in great danger on the sea I bring them back to you here; and sometimes I suffer shipwreck with the loss of all my goods, scarcely escaping alive."[67]

The young monk who could rattle this speech off in Latin would have had an impressive command of the language — not to mention basic economic theory, agricultural organisation, and current affairs. Complementing the drawings of the Julius Work Calendar, the wry and quizzical writings of Aelfric provide our richest insights into everyday English life in the year 1000 — including even its seafaring character. Viking raiding fleets may have been running rings round King Ethelred's attempts at naval defence, but there were clearly some Englishmen who saw themselves as people with a maritime heritage, for writing towards the end of Ethelred's reign, Aelfric looked back nostalgically to the years "when no fleet was ever heard of except of our own people who held this land."[68]

England's numerous seaports were proof of this heritage. *Port* was originally an Anglo-Saxon word that meant "market." The port reeve supervised the marketplace as the shire reeve supervised the shire. But by the tenth century the word also carried its modern meaning as a trading location on a harbour, and the array of English ports from Ipswich down to London and around the south coast was impressive. These centres of commerce significantly outnumbered the ports along the facing stretch of the Low Countries and northern France, and they were some of the fastest-growing communities in the country.

This reflected the fact that it was considerably easier to

travel and to transport merchandise in the year 1000 over water than over land. It was not until the eighteenth century that European engineers constructed highways to match the roads over which the Romans had transported their legions so efficiently. Hundreds of light wooden sail- and oar-powered boats shuttled up and down the rivers of medieval England in a network of navigable waterways that reached a surprising distance inland. The great royal residences were all built on or near water. Oxford and Cambridge were both ports before they were university towns, with busy trading jetties. Exeter, Worcester, Norwich, and Stamford also flourished on river traffic.

But the little ships that glided so busily between England's county towns did not fare so well on the open sea. Aelfric's "Merchant" was not exaggerating when he spoke of the risk of shipwreck. Nothing could be taken for granted. It was a matter of thanks to God if the narrow passage between Dover and Calais was accomplished without mishap. Accounts of Athelstan's army moving north against the Scots describe ships and men moving in tandem up the coast — and the navy would have stayed very safely within sight of land, for it was rare for a ship to spend a night on the open ocean if that could be avoided. Even the Vikings, the maestros of sea travel, who made up tents onboard and would travel through the night on their long ocean voyages, would come in to land after dark whenever they could. It was so much safer to make up fires and cook supper on a beach, or under the shelter of trees.[69]

Sea battles were always fought within sight of land. Engagements on the open sea required a scouting system that was not attempted until the time of King Henry V, and since medieval ships had no guns or missiles, fighting was a matter of hand-to-hand sword combat in sheltered inshore waters. Part of King Alfred's response to the Viking menace was a levy system whereby certain towns and localities were responsible for building and manning their own war-ship — the maritime equivalent of the fortified *burhs* — and the *Anglo-Saxon Chronicle* even credited Alfred with designing a new sort of ship to take on the Vikings. If it was anything like the Scandinavian longships that were harry-ing England in the ninth and tenth centuries, it was proba-bly some eighty feet long by fifteen feet wide — which was slightly narrower, but also slightly longer, than the seventy-five-foot-long *Santa Maria* in which Columbus crossed the Atlantic in 1492.

After many years of historical debate, we now know for certain that one summer around the year 1000, a Scandina-vian longship preceded Columbus to the New World by nearly five centuries, making landfall in Canada. For several generations, Norwegian sailors had been creeping west-wards around the top of the Atlantic, island-hopping first to Shetland and the Faroe Islands, then onwards to Iceland. The search was for pasture and timber, which took the explorers on to Greenland in the 980s, and then still further west, since the currents of the northern ocean were bringing driftwood over the horizon. The travellers may also have been following the cod, for it seems to have been the Viking technique of wind-drying cod on the prow of their ships that provided the nourishment the Norsemen needed to travel on round the coast of Baffin Island, Labrador, and

eventually to Newfoundland, which they named Vin-
land — because, as they boasted on their return, they had
found vines growing there.

This rosy description of a warm and fecund new world
was one of several reasons why later Icelandic accounts of
one Lief Eriksson reaching the other side of the Atlantic
sometime around the year 1000 were doubted by historians
for many years. But between 1961 and 1968 excavations at
L'Anse-aux-Meadows in Newfoundland uncovered cook-
ing pits, boathouses, metal ornaments, and some eight or
nine house sites of quite certainly Norse origin — along
with evidence of vine cultivation. The remains of the site
have been dated to within a few years of 1000 A.D., proving
that it was possible for the carpenters of the time to have
pinned, jointed, and tied several thousand pieces of wood
together with sufficient strength and flexibility to carry
men through the buffetings of the North Atlantic — while
also indicating that the men of the first millennium were
not, perhaps, the geographical dunces that later centuries
suggested.

It suited some thinkers in the eighteenth-century Age of
Reason to look down on the Middle Ages as a primitive and
backward time when men believed that the world was flat,
and that venturing too far away from Europe might entail
the risk of ships dropping over the edge. But King Alfred's
explanation of the solar system in one of the classical trans-
lations which he commissioned, and may even have carried
out himself, talks in unambiguously spherical terms, com-
paring the earth to "the yolk in the middle of an egg which
can move about [within the confines of] the egg. Similarly
the world remains still in its station. Outside, the play of

the waters, the sky, and the stars, and the bright shell itself revolve around it every day — long has it done so!"[70]

Alfred was obviously mistaken in his belief that the sky, stars, and "bright shell" of his egg travelled round the earth. That pre-Renaissance misconception was not corrected until the famous observations of Copernicus and Galileo. But the idea of the revolving heavens argued for similar roundness in the earth, and Alfred was clearly thinking in three-dimensional terms. When Charlemagne and the emperors of the time wanted to symbolise their earthly power, they put their hands upon an orb. Bede compared the earth to "the ball that boys play with," and when navigators in the year 1000 stood upon the prow of their ship, looking out at the curve of the horizon — both as it curved from left to right, and as it curved away from them — they drew the obvious conclusion. And to judge from Leif Eriksson, they were certainly not scared of sailing off the edge.

JULY

THE HUNGRY GAP

JULY WAS HAY MONTH IN THE YEAR 1000. It was the first great harvest of the year, a time of worry about the weather and the need to get the grass cut and dried before the rain could spoil it — and all to feed the animals, since the midsummer harvest produced no food for humans. Hay was fodder to keep the livestock going through the winter. So when the arduous work of haymaking was done, the medieval cultivator found himself facing another stretch that was harder still — the toughest month of the entire year, in fact, since the spring crops had not yet matured. The barns were at their lowest point and the grain bins could well be empty. Tantalisingly, on the very eve of the August harvest, people could find themselves starving in the balmiest month of all. July was the time of another phenomenon quite unknown to us in the modern West — "the hungry gap."[71]

In *Piers Plowman*, the late medieval fable of the land, we read how July was the month when the divide between rich and poor became most apparent. The rich could survive on the contents of their barns, and they had the money to pay the higher prices commanded by the dwindling stocks of food. Grain and bread prices could soar to exorbitant levels. But this scarcity made July the month when the poor learned the true meaning of poverty. As Piers sleeps in the fable, Patience comes to him in a dream, showing him how the poor suffer as they try to survive through their annual midsummer purgatory, grinding up the coarsest of wheat bran, and even old, shrivelled peas and beans to make some sort of bread.

Midsummer was also the season when that other sardonic observer of peasant life, the Flemish artist Pieter Breughel the Elder, painted his famous tableaux of crazed rural festivals. At the very end of the Middle Ages, Breughel depicted countryfolk wrapped up in fits of mass hysteria, and the historical accounts of these rural frenzies have explained the delirium in terms of the slender diet on which the poor had to subsist during the hungry gap. People were light-headed through lack of solid food, and modern chemistry has shown how the ergot that flowered on rye as it grew mouldy was a source of lysergic acid — LSD, the cult drug of the 1960s.

This hallucinogenic lift was accentuated by the hedgerow herbs and grains with which the dwindling stocks of conventional flour were amplified as the summer wore on. Poppies, hemp, and darnel were scavenged, dried, and ground up to produce a medieval hash brownie known as "crazy bread." So even as the poor endured hunger, it is possible that their diet provided them with some exotic and artificial paradises. "It was as if a spell had been placed on entire communities," according to one modern historian.[72] There are no accounts from the years around 1000 to match these descriptions of "colossal somnolent vertigo" which have been explained in terms of mind-bending substances, but who can tell? It is nice to think that, by accident or design, the poor of the year 1000 were tuning into transports of delight that matched the pleasures of their betters carousing in the great hall.

Social theory in the year 1000 divided the community into those who worked (the peasants, traders, and craftsmen), those who fought and administered justice (the kings and lords), and those who prayed. This last group obviously included, as it would today, the parish clergy with their pastoral duties of care to the laity. But in the Middle Ages there was an even larger group of holy folk who did nothing but pray — the men and women who had dedicated their entire lives to God, and had gone to live in monasteries. In the year 1000 there were thirty or so monasteries dotted across the English countryside from Carlisle in the north down to St. German's in Cornwall, and they were the economic centres of their communities.[73] They employed local labourers to work in their fields, but the monks carried out certain agricultural tasks themselves, since the combination of practical and spiritual was the essence of the monastic life as laid down by St. Benedict in the sixth century. Trying to formulate a routine that would keep good order in his own community of monks at Monte Cassino in southern Italy, Benedict produced a Rule that became the model for monasticism all over Christendom.

It was Benedictine monks who brought the word of God to England in 597. They ran the great cathedral churches at Canterbury, Rochester, Winchester, and Worcester. Their dormitories, refectories, libraries, and chapterhouses were part of the straggle of holy buildings that made up the religious campus around each cathedral, and their haunting plainsong chants set the tone of the services, echoing around the choirs and off the pillars of England's principal houses of God.

The chant was the heartbeat of religious devotion in England in the year 1000. It was the channel by which man spoke to his God, either directly or by catching the ear of Mary or one of the saints. Its rhythmic beauty was an act of homage as well as an enticement to the divine listener, and as each monk made his music, he knew that he was practising for the glorious day when he would stand as a member of one of the choirs of angels in Heaven, and raise his voice in the very presence of God Himself.

The chanting of the liturgy was one of the centralising forces of Christendom. Today it is usually referred to as the Gregorian chant, from the tradition that it was developed by Pope Gregory the Great — the same Gregory who dispatched missionaries to England — and one can certainly imagine the good Pope singing with Augustine and his companions as they dedicated themselves for their mission to the distant islands of the northwest. But there is no evidence that Gregory himself was particularly involved in the collecting together of these mesmerising melodies which had their roots in the Hebrew chants that were taken over and adapted by the first Christians. The chant was the product of practice and elaboration by the countless churchmen and women of the first millennium whose lives were given meaning by this inspiring and transcendent sound.

The chant uplifted people spiritually — and it provided physical uplift as well. The decades following the year 1000

saw a significant growth in the building of monastic infirmaries, which were medical institutions in the modern
sense of the word, but also offered refuge to the old and
dying, as well as accommodation for travellers and pilgrims.
"Let all guests who come to the monastery be entertained
like Christ Himself," wrote St. Benedict, "because He will
say, 'I was a stranger and you took me in.'"[74] Many of these
infirmaries were built on deeply symbolic thoroughfares,
beside bridges or rivers, or much-travelled roads, and
though they could offer rest and seclusion and simple herbal
remedies to those who were sick, the main constituent of
their healing regimen was the primeval resonance of the
Mass and the deeply affecting rhythms of the chant.

The monks rose in the middle of the night to sing their
first prayers. Signing up for the monastic life meant saying
goodbye forever to a full night's sleep, since two hours after
midnight was the time set for the night office. Many
monastic buildings had a staircase that went straight down
from the dormitory into the chapel to ease the pain of going
from sleep to their work of prayer in the cold and dark of a
winter's night. This service in the small hours was called
Matins, and afterwards the community went back to bed
and slept again for three hours, before rising for good at
6 o'clock to sing Prime. Five other prayer times punctuated
the day — Tierce, Sext, None, Vespers, and Compline,
which was said at 7.00 P.M. in winter and 8.00 P.M. in summer, after which everyone went straight to bed.

Study and contemplation were the guiding themes of
monastic life between prayer times. Every refectory had a
pulpit or lectern from which one of the brethren would
read while his comrades ate in silence — and a document

of the time sets out the signals and sign language with which the monks were taught to communicate in the absence of speech. St. Benedict insisted in his Rule that monks should be silent for as much of the day and night as possible, but he also ordained that they could communicate with signs, and the details of these signals have come down to us through an Anglo-Saxon manual of monastic sign language from the cathedral at Canterbury.

The manual was almost certainly produced in the same Canterbury writing studio as the Julius Work Calendar, and at about the same time, and it provides some rich insights not only into the lives of monks, but into many practical details of daily existence in the years around 1000 A.D.[75] So you would like a little wine? "Then make with your two fingers as if you were undoing the tap of a cask." Pass the butter? "Stroke with three fingers on the inside of your hand." A little pepper perhaps? "Knock with one index finger on the other." Salt? "Shake your hands with your three fingers together, as if you were salting something." Reading the 127 different signs set out in *Monasteriales Indicia*, one gets the impression that mealtimes in a Benedictine refectory were rather like a gathering of baseball coaches, all furiously beckoning, squeezing their ear lobes, meaningfully rubbing their fingers up and down the sides of their noses, and smoothing their hands over their stomachs.

We learn of the hierarchy inside the monastery. The sign for the abbot was to put two fingers to one's head and take hold of a hank of hair, as if tugging the forelock — and indicating, perhaps, that below the bald patch of the tonsure, monks grew their hair quite long. The provost, or bursar, was indicated by a single index finger raised over the head, the sign of the ox, because he was the provider of such things, while the cellarer was indicated by a circular turning of the hand and wrist, as if unlocking a door with a key. The sign for the "master of the boys" (putting two fingers to one's eyes and holding up the little finger) reminds us that the monasteries were educational establishments — the only schools in the England of 1000 A.D. — and also suggests how the learned and humorous Aelfric of Cerne Abbas would have been referred to by his colleagues. Signs 47 and 48, however, also provide a reminder of how Aelfric would have kept discipline in the classroom, since these two instructions explain how to call for the cane or the scourge — the cat o' nine tails — in accordance with St. Benedict's instruction: "Let the abbot restrain the badly behaved, and the inflexible and proud, or the disobedient, with blows or chastisement of the body."

More than half a dozen gestures for different types of candle, taper, wick, lantern, and lamp bear witness to a world lit only by fire. Signs for a bedcover and a pillow ("Stroke the sign of a feather inside your left hand") suggest that the monks slept quite comfortably between prayer times, while signs 91 and 92 make clear that the brethren put on both slippers and socks when they rose in the night to go down to the chapel. Sign 102 ("Stroke with your two hands up your thigh") tells us that the brothers wore underpants under their black Benedictine habits.

Towards the end of the manual are two signs that refer to the king and to the king's wife, and it might seem strange that tenth-century monks received instruction in how to hold their hands over their heads with all their fingers splayed out in the shape of a crown (sign 118 — king), or to stroke their scalps in a circular fashion and then pat their pates (sign 119 — queen). But these secular signals help explain why English monasteries were so healthy in the year 1000. The entire generation of monastic settlement inspired by St. Augustine and his successors in the seventh century was wiped out by the Vikings in the waves of attacks that were finally checked and reversed by King Alfred in the 890s, and it was only in the tenth century that there had been a rebirth of the monasteries. This had been accomplished by an alliance between the church and the crown, symbolised by the solemn anointing of King Edgar at his coronation in 973, the first time that a king of all England had been blessed with this sacrament that was jealously reserved by the Roman church. The kings of Scotland had to wait for it until 1331. The coronation of Edgar raised English kings to the level of emperors, and it initiated the mystical and sometimes almost sacerdotal status with which the English royal family was to wreath itself for centuries to come.

It was a two-way deal, since Edgar was anxious to assert his royal authority, while Dunstan of Canterbury and other reform-minded clerics were keen to revitalise the church. So the bishops inserted prayers for the royal family in their liturgies, while the royal family deeded lands to the church, thus enhancing the grandeur of England's cathedrals, and also making it possible to reestablish a network of monastic settlements across the land. All of England's monasteries in the year 1000 had been founded or refounded in the previous fifty years. Crown and church had a common interest in strengthening national respect for institutions of authority, and the monasteries were the crucial factor in fostering

Alfred's secret ingredient for national success: the monks spread knowledge through their schools, and they also amplified knowledge through their effective monopoly over the written word.

In the scriptorium, or writing studio, of every monastery the brethren dipped their sharpened goose quills into their phials of coloured acid and bent over their transcriptions of ancient manuscripts. The writing stand of each monk held two books, the manuscript on which the scribe was working and the volume from which he was copying, for to be learned in the year 1000 was to copy. You did not innovate. You learned by absorbing and reproducing the wisdom of earlier authorities.

It does not seem creative by modern standards, this relentless consigning of old authorities to the deep-freeze cabinet, but the monasteries of the first millennium were creating the cultural Noah's Ark on which our own understanding of the past is based. It is thanks to their copying — and to the documents preserved by the Arabs who controlled the Mediterranean — that we can today read the words of Plato and Aristotle or Julius Caesar. And from copying came, slowly, what we would nowadays describe as creativity.

The Julius Work Calendar is an example of this. There are similar calendars dating from late Roman times in which each month is illustrated with a particular practical task, and the lilting, sing-song text of the Julius calendar of 1020 can be traced back a century earlier to the reign of Ethelred's great-uncle, King Athelstan. Sometime in the 920s, the king, who inherited his grandfather Alfred's love of books, commissioned some work on a beautiful psalter —

an illuminated book of the psalms — which had found its way into the royal library from the diocese of Liège in the Low Countries.

Athelstan seems to have decided to enlarge and personalise this handsome volume from Liège with a metrical calendar of the saints, and thus came about the earliest surviving version of the 365 lines of verse that later found their way into the Julius Work Calendar. Athelstan's list of saints' days had no illustrations, however, and the list of feast days included an unusual number of saints that were associated with the Pas de Calais, the long-settled farming area just across the English Channel. This suggested that the poem itself, or the scribe who composed it, came from northern France,[76] though his list of saints also included a surprising number of Irish saints and feast days. This added to the confusion — to the modern way of thinking at least — but this was the essence of the medieval system of learning through precedent and accretion: a beautiful Flemish book of psalms, embellished with a list of saints from northern France, turned into verse, quite possibly, by an Irish monk, or a scribe who was looking at a list of saints from Ireland — and all this under the patronage of an English king in Winchester.

A hundred years later, the Julius Work Calendar took the process of elaboration one stage further. Perhaps Canterbury borrowed the Athelstan Psalter, with its 365 lines of verse, under one of the many exchange schemes by which England's newly reestablished monasteries lent each other texts to reconstitute their libraries. We know that Canterbury happened to possess in these years another beautiful illuminated document, the so-called Utrecht Psalter, created around 830 in the diocese of Rheims in northern France, and characterised by vivid and almost impressionistic sketches of daily life. These lifelike drawings took their theme from ancient illustrations, and later versions had brought the classical prototype up to date with such contemporary details as the latest weapons and farm implements, as well as current fashions in clothing.

The novelty of the sketches in the Utrecht Psalter was clearly the inspiration of the dramatic line drawings that bring such life to the Julius Work Calendar. We can imagine the Canterbury scribe with the old rhyming catalogue of saints from Winchester on his copying stand. What could he do to enhance the list and make it particular to Canterbury, the headquarters of the English church? Somewhere in the writing studio were lying the parchment leaves of the Utrecht Psalter, quite possibly unbound at that date, so their catchy, challenging, and very modern style of sketching could also be propped up in front of him. Outside in the southern English countryside, where he was expected to work regularly as part of his monastic duties, were the haymakers swinging their scythes. So the scribe set to work sketching, catching the fatigue and sweat on the brow of the bald-headed reaper pausing for breath on the right hand side of his July drawing, while, on the other side, another of the reapers stood back to sharpen his scythe with his honing stone. Today we admire the drawings of this talented but unknown artist for what they tell us about life in early eleventh-century England, but his fellow scribes and monks probably praised his illustrations for their rootedness in the tradition of the Utrecht original, with all its classical precedents.

The glory of medieval manuscripts lies in the drawings which are aptly described as illumination. Their sense of colour and sinuous inventiveness bring light to what would otherwise seem dark and routine — and that is certainly the case with the sketches of the Julius Work Calendar, which have no added colour at all. Their life derives from the vigour of their line and from their sharpness of observation. Look at the drawing for the month of May, with the baby lamb suckling its mother. On the hillside beside the sheep the two shepherds lean together chatting, deep in gossip and conversation, while one of them scratches the back of his head. This is reportage based on firsthand observation. The drawing for the month of February shows the pruner tackling the tree on the left by cutting *upwards* from below, which was the correct way to lop off a heavy branch.

To the modern eye these drawings are secular. There are no halos or crosses. There is absolutely nothing other-worldly about them, for while the words of the calendar are looking heavenwards, these drawings focus on man in a profoundly humanist fashion — and on that group of men who, for the most part, occupied the humblest and least privileged ranks of society.

It must be assumed that the monk who illustrated the Julius Work Calendar with such lively interest and compassion was a believer. *Everybody* believed in the year 1000 — especially the pagans and those whom the church condemned as heretics. The sin of the heretic was to believe the wrong thing. But the modern viewer can sense a change of emphasis in these very human monthly labours. There is something of the agnostic detachment which was to alter the unquestioning nature of medieval thought in the next five hundred years. In this old and very traditional document we can sense the beginning of the probing and sceptical spirit that would bring the Middle Ages to the triumphant climax of the Renaissance and also inspire the ages of exploration and science.

AUGUST

REMEDIES

AUGUST 1, LAMMAS DAY, IS ONE OF the oldest English country festivals. Shakespeare's Juliet had her birthday "come Lammas eve at night," and to this day Lammas is one of the quarter-days in Scotland's financial year. Lammas sounds as if it had its origins in some sort of religious festival deriving from "lamb" and "mass," but its origin was actually the annual Anglo-Saxon round of farming and survival. Lammas was *hlaf-maesse*, loaf-mass, the day when the hungry gap ended and the first loaf could be made from the new harvest. "I must sustain myself till Lammas when I hope to have harvest in my barn," declared Piers Plowman. "Then I can have the kind of meal I like."[77]

The Julius Work Calendar drawing for August makes clear that harvesting for the loaf-mass was an activity that involved the whole community. No less than seven labourers, more than in any other drawing in the cycle, are gathered together, busily sweeping their sickles, cutting the wheat, binding it into sheaves, and loading it into another neatly carpentered Saxon cart. "Ten hours of darkness, fourteen hours of daylight," noted the calendar's hour count for August, and every single working hour of the month was filled with urgency, since the bread harvest was the very fulcrum of survival. More than meat, milk, or any type of vegetable, bread was the staff of life for people in the year 1000. "I make people's hearts strong," boasted the "Baker" in Aelfric's *Colloquy*. "I am the stamina of men."[78]

The bread of the early Middle Ages was round, coarse, and quite flat by modern standards, not baked in a tin, with the texture of a pita bread, nan, or chapati today. The natural gluten in wheat bread provided a "raising" agent which gave it more air than bread made with rye or barley, but it was probably quite old and tough by the time most people ate it, since outside the towns and the monasteries there were few specialised bakers producing fresh bread every day. Country people must have regularly eaten bread that was a week or more old, softening the crust by dipping it into the gruel-like pottage of grain and vegetables which was the plain but healthy staple of the Englishman's diet. In Central Europe the peasants ate rye bread, but in England wheat was the grain of choice, and barley was definitely judged second-best. Saints demonstrated their humility by eating barley bread, and one hagiography relates how the emperor Julian took offence at being offered barley bread by St. Basil. "Barley is only fit for horses," declared the emperor indignantly, and offered the holy man some grass in return.[79]

Grain was ground into flour in one of the recently constructed watermills. When the Normans carried out their 1086 Domesday inventory of the land they had conquered, they discovered that England contained 5,624 watermills, just about one for every village and hamlet, and many of these must have been in operation by the year 1000. The mill, like the plough team, was a communal facility that the village operated jointly, adding sophistication to the economy, and providing yet another incentive for people to make use of cash. The mill wheels were generally built of oak, the internal gear wheels of elm, with power transmitted through a solid oak shaft banded with iron as reinforcement. Turning only slowly, the early medieval watermill put-putted along with the horsepower of a modern moped or small motorbike.[80]

August was the month when flies started to become a problem, buzzing round the dung heaps in the corner of every farmyard and hovering over the open cesspits of human refuse that were located outside every house. If the late twentieth century is scented with gasolene vapour and exhaust fumes, the year 1000 was perfumed with shit. Cow dung, horse manure, pig and sheep droppings, chicken shit — each variety of excrement had its own characteristic bouquet, from the sweet smell of the vegetable eater to the acrid edge of gut-processed meat, requiring the human nose of the year 1000 to function as a considerably less prissy organ than ours today.

There are modern archaeological experts who study excreta intensively, rummaging through the latrine pits of ancient settlements to discover such fundamental details as the fact that the toilet paper of the year 1000 was moss. "Coprolite" is their name for the humble turd, from "copros," the Greek word for dung, and thanks to their familiarity with the size and shape of their dried and mineralised quarry, they have discovered that the medieval English-man's best friend was his dog — whose droppings have varied little in appearance in the course of a thousand years. Human stools, on the other hand, have not often survived in a similarly cohesive form, suggesting that bowels in the year 1000 were subject to significantly looser motions than they are today. Recurring gut infections and a diet with a high vegetable content are the likely reasons for this, though the presence in the latrine pits of animal bone frag-ments and painful-looking herring, eel, and stickleback spines suggest that our ancestors were well supplied with protein. The frequency of apple pips, plum and cherry stones also suggests that, when it came to fruit, medieval men and women did not let a morsel go to waste.

The siting of the latrine pits of the first millennium shows how imperfectly people understood the basic rules of cleanliness and health. Plans that survive from a later period show that monasteries worked out a sensible and sanitary location for their *necessarium* — their Latin contribution to history's list of euphemisms for the smallest room. The monks were careful to site their latrines over running water, and to choose positions for their monasteries that gave access to drinking water that was unpolluted by that stream. Plans for the French monastery of Cluny show a guest wing with seventy beds and an adjoining latrine with seventy separate stalls.[81]

But few other people operated so fastidiously. Both in vil-lages and towns, the latrine was sited at or near the back-door of most houses, with no apparent concern for the odour, nor for the flies that had so little distance to travel from the refuse to the food that people ate. There was no awareness of how disease can be spread by bacteria, and people took it for granted that their bodies should provide hospitality for parasites that ranged from the relatively inoffensive whipworm to the more sinister maw-worm, which could grow as long as 30 centimetres, migrating all over the body, including the lungs and the liver. The maw-worm could emerge unexpectedly from any orifice, including, most alarmingly, the corners of people's eyes.

The flea was a parasite towards which people were less tolerant, since it nipped its host quite nastily, and remedies for dealing with the nuisance were much canvassed. One late medieval survey ran the gamut of options, from locking flea-ridden garments inside an airtight chest, to laying down sheepskins around a flea-infested bed so that when the insects jumped out, they would show up black against the white background.[82] At this point, presumably, the medieval flea hunter leaped forward with a cudgel, heavy cloth, or the equivalent of a rolled-up newspaper, to beat the insects to death.

The modern remedy for fleas and grubbiness — a good scrub of the body crevices — did not not accord with the medieval mentality. The regulations of one tenth-century European monastery prescribed five baths for every monk per year, but that was fanaticism by Anglo-Saxon standards of personal hygiene. One later commentator derided the Danish practice of bathing and combing the hair every Saturday, but did admit that this seemed to improve Danish chances with the womenfolk.[83] The thatched roof, rough organic walls, and beaten-earth floor of the medieval house provided a myriad of refuges for insects and bacteria. There were no modern "working surfaces" that could be washed down in an antiseptic fashion. Indeed, there was no concept of antiseptic at all. If a morsel of food fell off your plate, the advice of one contemporary document was to pick it up, make the sign of the cross over it, season it well — and then eat it.[84]

The sign of the cross was the antiseptic of the year 1000. The person who dropped his food on the floor knew that he was taking some sort of risk when he picked it up and put it in his mouth, but he trusted in his faith. Today we have faith in modern medicine, though few of us can claim much personal knowledge of how it actually works, and we also know that the ability to combat quite major illnesses can be affected by what we call "a positive state of mind" — what the Middle Ages experienced as "faith."

The comparison may not seem exact. Hygiene is hygiene, and no amount of positive thinking can spare you the consequences of eating contaminated meat. Nor do we need to understand the technicalities of modern medicine, it could be argued, to draw the obvious lesson from the numbers of sick people who trust themselves to modern medicine and are cured. But the believer in the year 1000 could point to the Bible, which listed no less than thirty-five miracles in which Jesus defeated illness through the power of faith, and every believer knew that the saints were keeping that miraculous tradition alive. Aelfric described the tangible evidence of St. Swithin's healing touch in Winchester as the millennium approached: "The old church was hung all round with crutches (from one end to the other, on either wall), and with the stools of cripples who had been healed there, and not even so could they put half of them up."[85]

While people had no knowledge of modern germ theory in the year 1000, they were well aware of the contagiousness of diseases. Leprosy was a European illness in those days, and the eleventh and twelfth centuries saw a dramatic growth in the construction of charitable leper hospitals, partly to take care of the victims, but principally to confine them safely away from the rest of the population. History records how the Roman church at one stage became suspicious of human dissection and sought to ban anatomy lessons, but that was a later development. In the year 1000, the internal workings of the body had been explored and were understood as thoroughly as people knew that the world was not flat. A much-copied ninth-century manuscript, now in the Royal Library of Brussels, shows thirteen anatomical drawings illustrating the positions that the foetus could adopt in the womb.[86] These must have been based on practical, obstetrical observation, as surely as this description of foetal development from an eleventh-century Anglo-Saxon document in the library at Canterbury: "In the sixth week the brain is covered with a membrane on the outside; in the second month the veins are formed . . . and the blood then flows into the feet and into the hands, and he is then articulated in limbs and altogether developed; in the third month he is man, except for the soul"[87] — which meant, presumably, that abortion could carry no ethical connotations before the fourth month.

Cemetery excavations in several corners of England have to date revealed thirteen Anglo-Saxon skulls that have been pierced with neatly drilled holes, and nine of these show evidence of subsequent bone healing, which removes the possibility that this trepanning was part of some sinister sacrificial or posthumous ritual. Today trepanning is carried out as a surgical treatment after head injuries. Drilling through the skull can relieve the pressure created by a bruised and swollen brain, and this may have been the reason why these thirteen Anglo-Saxons underwent this dramatic but comparatively safe therapy. The modern doctor deploys the surgical equivalent of a Black & Decker power drill to pierce the skull, and in the year 1000 the trepanner had at his disposal the semi-mechanical bow drill that was used by the carpenters and masons of the time. Known to the Romans, the bow drill had a sharp metal bit that was turned alternately to and fro by a strap wrapped around a wooden handle, on the same principle as the overhead pole lathe — so we can assume that, even in the absence of anaesthetic, the trepanned Anglo-Saxon experienced comparatively little discomfort from the procedure.

We should not, however, take the analogy with modern medicine any further, since there is little likelihood that medieval trepanning was carried out on the basis of any physical diagnosis that we would recognise today. It was, more probably, executed as an exorcism to free the soul of what was seen as affliction by evil spirits. Devils, elves, and spirits were the other side of a medicine in which sufferers believed they could be made better through divine intervention, for if it was God who provided cures for illness, it was logical to assume that the Devil had caused the trouble in the first place.

The Anglo-Saxon identified elves as the Devil's particular lieutenants in the mortification of the body. People spoke of "elf-shot" as we today would talk of germs, explaining infection as something that had been caused by an invisible arrow or dart fired off by some malevolent sprite — and the logic of that was that an arrow should feature in the cure. If you suffered from a stitch in your side or from a particularly bad pain, one tenth-century German remedy recommended placing an arrowhead or some other piece of metal on the sore spot, and then uttering this charm:"Come out, worm, with nine little worms, out from the marrow into the bone, from the bone into the flesh, from the flesh into the skin, from the skin into this arrow."[88] And just in case this invocation sounded pagan, the sufferer was told to add the prayer:"So be it, Lord."

An English charm against a wen, or lump on the skin, addressed the wen as if it were a person — and as if it belonged to a clan of related lumps that extended from small bodily extrusions to the hills on the horizon. Could the awkward body lump now please pack its bags and go back home to its family in the mountains?

Wen, Wen, little Wen,
here you must not build, here have no abode
but you must go north to the nearby hill
where, poor wretch, you have a brother.
He will lay a leaf at your head.
Under the paw of the wolf, under the eagle's wing,
under the claw of the eagle, may you ever decline!
Shrink like coal on the hearth!
Wizen like filth on the wall!
Waste away like water in the pail!
Become as small as a grain of linseed,
and far smaller than a hand-worm's hip-bone and so very small
that you are at last nothing at all.

Anglo-Saxon charms were literally charming. Cajoling and gently humorous, they had a friendliness and empathy with nature which may have provided tenth- and eleventh-century invalids with the most healing impulse of all. Successful medicine has several components, and one can find them all set out in a tenth-century Winchester document known as "Bald's Leechbook" — "Leechbook" meaning medicine book because of the medieval reliance on leeches for medicinal purposes, and Bald being the otherwise unknown owner of the book whose name was inscribed on the title page.

The manuscript shows that this was very much a working manual. With its practical drawings and commentaries in a later hand, it could almost be Dr. Bald's Casebook, and its remedies were conveniently listed in descending order from the head to the toe. One cure for a headache involved binding the stalk of the herb crosswort to the head with a red bandana, while chilblains were to be treated with a mixture of eggs, wine, and fennel root. Right in the middle of the remedies, along with other ministrations to the groin area, was listed the Viagra of the year 1000 — the yellow-flowered herb agrimony. Boiled in milk, agrimony was guaranteed to excite the man who was "insufficiently virile" — and if boiled in Welsh ale, it was described as having exactly the contrary effect.

Bald's remedy for shingles revealed the Anglo-Saxon's connoisseurship of trees, since the potion involved bark from no less than fifteen different varieties: aspen, apple, maple, elder, willow, sallow, myrtle, wych-elm, oak, blackthorn, birch, olive, dogwood, ash-tree, and the quickbeam or mountain ash. The presence of such Mediterranean

woods as olive reflected the Leechbook's reliance on classical authorities like Pliny, and suggests that olive bark and
other such exotic panaceas must have been traded in Lombardy and packed into the English saddlebags along with
pepper and spices.

A number of the ingredients in the Leechbook had hallucinogenic qualities, suggesting that the potions were designed as palliatives to make the patient feel pleasantly high
without any remedial effect — medieval morphine, rather
like the "skin of frog" cited in Shakespeare's famous witches'
brew in *Macbeth*, which has been shown to possess definitely psychedelic properties. *Macbeth*, the play, was, of
course, written in the early 1600s, but King Macbeth himself was a real-life character, born sometime around 1000
A.D. with a wife to whom the chronicles give the name of
Gruoc. Macbeth ruled Scotland from around 1040 to 1057,
and spent much of his reign keeping the Vikings out of
Scotland with more success than Ethelred enjoyed to the
south.

Several of the Leechbook recipes would have done credit
to the witches in *Macbeth*. Spider bite could be cured with
fried and crushed black snails; lower-back pain was said to
respond to the smoke of smouldering goat's hair, while
baldness could certainly be removed by applying an oint-
ment from the ashes of burned bees. Modern research has
failed to confirm that these recipes contained ingredients of
any medicinal significance. But their bizarre rarity must
have impressed practitioners and patients in the same way
that rhinoceros horn and lamb's foetus do the trick for some
today, and the Leechbook was by no means devoid of medical understanding. It explained the operation of the liver in

modern textbook style: "It casts out the impurities which are there and collects the pure blood and sends it through four arteries, chiefly to the heart."

Bald's prescription for dysentery showed a particularly well-balanced combination of folk remedy, religious conviction, and tender loving care — which probably constituted the most efficacious ingredient in the recipe: "Take a bramble of which both ends are in the earth, take the newer root, dig it up, and cut nine chips on your left hand, then sing three times: *Miserere mei deus* [Psalm 56] and nine times the Our Father. Take then mugwort and everlasting and boil these three in several kinds of milk until they become red. Let him then sup a good bowl full of it, fasting at night, sometime before he takes other food. Make him rest in a soft bed and wrap him up warm. If more is necessary, do so again; if you still need it then, do so a third time. It will not be necessary to do so more often."

The medical theory on which the Leechbook and much Anglo-Saxon medicine was based was the ancient classical concept of the four bodily fluids — blood, phlegm, red choler or bile, and black bile — which were believed to parallel the natural elements of fire, water, air, and earth, and which combined in the body in varying proportions to create varying emotional and physical make-ups, or "humours": "When blood predominates," explained Bede, "it makes people joyful and glad, sociable, laughing and talking a great deal. Red cholic makes them thin, though eating much, swift, bold, wrathful, agile. Black cholic makes them serious of settled disposition, even sad. Phlegm renders them slow, sleepy, forgetful."[89]

The shifting tide of these humours was seasonal. "Blood-letting is to be avoided for a fortnight before Lammas," commanded the Leechbook, "and for thirty-five days afterwards, because then all poisonous things fly and injure men greatly." At these times of year, counselled the manual, the Englishman should not go out in the midday sun, but should follow the example of the Romans and the southern races who built themselves houses with thick earthen walls that would shelter them from "the air's heat and poisonousness."[90]

The theory of the four humours attributed fevers and many other disorders to an excessive build-up of blood in the body, and the removal of that "bad blood" played a major role in the medical practices of the year 1000. The application of leeches and the slicing open of veins were standard treatment for conditions that ranged from life-threatening illness to simply feeling out of sorts — and it is difficult to see the justification for this gruesome and debilitating remedy, which weakened the body beyond any perverse psychological tonic that its suffering might have inspired. Modern doctors nod benignly at some of the remedies and principles in Bald's Leechbook, but none has a good word to say for bloodletting — nor for cautery, the other medieval method of balancing the humours.

Cautery involved the applying of red-hot iron pokers to different parts of the anatomy in an excruciatingly painful version of acupuncture. One ninth-century Italian manuscript details the points on the body to which the hot iron should be applied, and shows the physician holding up a drinking goblet in an apparent promise of relief from the pain. It is the earliest known European illustration of a medical procedure, and the presence of some attempt at anaesthetic is comforting. But the potion — which must have been a strong sleeping draft or its opposite, a stimulant or hallucinogen — can only have mitigated the agony. It all sounds hopelessly primitive to us, but the modern techniques by which microcameras and lasers enable surgeons to enter the body through the smallest of incisions already offer some indication of how future generations are likely to look back on the gall bladder operations and appendix scars of the twentieth century.

As one studies the array of remedies and medical treatment that was available to the sick in the year 1000, one would hardly blame the patient who foreswore human intervention and decided to let nature take its course. As Aelfric sagely put it: "He that is sick, let him pray for his health to the Lord God, and endure the pain patiently." [91]

SEPTEMBER

PAGANS AND PANNAGE

W ITH A STIRRING TOOT ON THEIR hunting horn, these two Anglo-Saxon adventurers are heading into the woods in search of big game — though to judge from the herd of pigs munching tranquilly in the undergrowth, the hunters may not get much of a chase. There were some wild boar in the forests of England in the year 1000, as there were a few surviving wolves, but much more numerous were the herds of free-range pigs which roamed the woodlands. Villagers started to cull the pigs as September heralded the beginning of winter, and it is quite possible that these boar chasers with their long spears and greyhound may simply come home with the slowest and most wobbly old sow in the herd.

Once the harvest had been gathered in early medieval times, every farmer and householder had to work out the basic equation of survival through the winter. How long would the larder last, and which animals looked like consuming more fodder than their life expectancy could justify? September was the month when ailing and elderly livestock was turned into sausages and pies, and the pig was the crucial factor in this calculation. The cultivated harvest in the fields was matched by the woodland "mast" of beech-nuts, acorns, chestnuts, and other fruits of the forest. Autumn was when the hogs were at their fattest.

You could make use of virtually every bit of the medieval pig, which, foraging alongside and sometimes mating with its wild cousins, had a distinctly boar-like appearance. Its snout was long and aggressive, and it had long legs. Hung in the rafters for a month or so, its sides of bacon made a virtue of the smoke that hung heavy in the thick and pungent atmosphere of the Anglo-Saxon home. Its stomach lining provided tripe. Its intestines provided skin for sausages, and its blood was the main ingredient for black pudding. Sheep, cattle, and poultry all made multiple contributions to the economy of the rural household, but the omnivorous pig was the most versatile and least trouble of all. "Pannage" was the term for the natural, self-foraging diet with which pigs sustained themselves in the Middle Ages, and the value of medieval woodland was often expressed in terms of how many pigs that sector of forest could support.

Farm animals were distinctly smaller in the year 1000 than they are today — and they were also smaller than they had been six centuries earlier. The Romans had worked systematically on improving the yield of their meat crop with relatively scientific livestock breeding programmes, but the Anglo-Saxons did not bother. Archaeological excavations show the bones of cows, pigs, and sheep getting progressively smaller through the centuries, then getting bigger again with the introduction of scientific husbandry in the later Middle Ages. In the years around 1000, a plough team of eight oxen was needed to break up virgin land. By the fifteenth century, four to six better-bred beasts were enough[92] — though this also reflected improvements in plough technology.

The Anglo-Saxons loved their animals. Just as they could recognise the livestock of their neighbours, the chances were they had a pet name for every creature in their own extended family, and they would have revelled in the anthropomorphic menagerie of Walt Disney. Their poems took delight in attributing human characteristics like steadfastness and cunning to the members of the animal kingdom, seeing them as fellow occupants of a world in which human and animal interests were intermingled. Mother Nature's children were all their brothers and sisters.

September was the month when the orchard yielded its richest harvest. *Orceard* was an Anglo-Saxon word derived from *Weortyeard*, a garden or plant yard. Archbishop Wulfstan's account of the well-run estate describes fruit grafting as one of the annual tasks, and another manuscript of the time indicates that plums were developed at Glastonbury by grafting onto the rootstock of the native sloe bush.[93] Monastic communities were particularly well placed to exchange fruit grafts and plant clippings in the same way that they exchanged books for their libraries. The abbey at Ely was famous for its vineyards, as well as for its orchards and a plant nursery which cultivated several varieties of fruit trees.[94]

Apple, pear, plum, fig, quince, peach, and mulberry trees all featured in the garden plan of one grand monastery designed, though never actually built, for Ireland's missionary monks on the shores of Lake Constance in Switzerland.[95] St. Benedict's command that monks should not consume meat was interpreted by most communities to mean meat from red-blooded, four-legged animals, so poultry was considered immune from the prohibition, as were rabbits, which the Normans brought to England after 1066. But the monastic diet still tended to the noncarnivorous, with a high dairy content and a healthy proportion of nuts. The monks of St. Gall planned to grow chestnuts, almonds, hazelnuts, and walnuts on their estate, and when it came to vegetables, their kitchen garden made allowance for onions, leeks, celery, radish, carrots, garlic, shallots, parsnip, cabbage, parsley, dill, chervil, marigold, coriander, poppy, and lettuce.

These fruits and vegetables were almost certainly more tasty than their modern equivalents, but, like the livestock of the year 1000, they were considerably smaller. Even when allowance has been made for withering and shrinkage, the fruit pips and seeds discovered in early English archaeological sites are smaller than those of today — and several staples that we take for granted in our modern diet are noticeable for their absence.

There was no spinach. This did not appear in European gardens until spinach seeds were brought back from the Crusades in the twelfth century. Broccoli, cauliflower, runner beans, and brussels sprouts were all developed in later centuries by subsequent generations of horticulturalists. Nor were there any potatoes or tomatoes. Europe had to wait five centuries for those, until the exploration of the Americas, and though the recipe books describe warm possets and herbal infusions, there were none of the still-to-be-imported stimulants — tea, coffee, or chocolate.

The greatest dietary gap by modern standards was the absence of any type of sugar. Venetian records describe a shipment of sugar cane reaching Venice for the first time in 996 A.D., probably from Persia or Egypt,[96] but sugar was not imported any further into Europe until the end of the Middle Ages,[97] and it did not swamp the European palate, creating the modern sweet tooth, until the development of the Caribbean sugar plantations of the seventeenth century. Anglo-Saxon skeletal remains are remarkable for the relative absence of dental and jaw decay.

Honey was the principal source of sweetness in the year 1000. It was so precious it was almost a currency in medieval England. People paid taxes with it, and it was a lucky day when a swarm of bees settled in your thatch:

> Christ, there is a swarm of bees outside,
> Fly hither, my little cattle,
> In blest peace, in God's protection,
> Come home safe and sound!

The church devised this prayer to help the faithful take advantage of the opportunity, and it developed into quite a lengthy invocation:

> Sit down, sit down, bee!
> St. Mary commanded thee!
> Thou shalt not have leave,
> Thou shalt not fly to the wood.
> Thou shalt not escape me,
> Nor go away from me.
> Sit very still,
> Wait God's will![98]

Bees did not produce only honey. Propolis, the reddish resin used by worker bees as a building material, provided a healing balm that was greatly prized for the treatment of wounds — while a measure of beeswax commanded an even higher price than an equivalent measure of honey. Beeswax made the best candles, which shone with a bright and steady light, exuding a pleasant smell that was infinitely preferable to the aroma of a guttering tallow candle made from mutton fat.

"Take some earth," ran another recipe for claiming a swarm of bees. "Sprinkle it with thy right hand under thy right foot and say: 'I hold it under foot; I have found it!'"

This was a pagan charm, an ancient precursor and rival to the prayer devised by the church, and its opening words established the owner's claim to the swarm in the same way that the modern rugby player digs his heel into the ground when he catches the ball and shouts "Mark!"

The next stage was to cast a handful of grit or gravel over the swarm and cry out:

> Stay, victorious women, sink to earth!
> Never fly wild to the wood.
> Be as mindful of my good
> as each man is of food and home.[99]

The medieval beekeeper may have believed that the bees actually heard his words and understood them, but a modern beekeeper's explanation of the charm's effectiveness is that bees are genetically programmed to cluster round the queen and to take her down to earth in a protective bundle when they sense danger — be it in a storm of hail or in a scattering of grit cast by a predatory Anglo-Saxon.[100] When it came to bee husbandry, the English had made considerable advances over the Romans, who presumed that the chief bee in any hive must be a male. The Romans also believed that when bees swarmed, they were setting off to war against some rival hive. The Anglo-Saxons, however, had worked out that the chief bee in every colony was a female, and they also understood that when bees swarmed it was a matter of proliferation and the creation of another colony.

In the absence of honey, another source of sweetness was the crushed pulp of grapes left over from the making of wine. The Normans' Domesday survey of 1086 listed no less than thirty-eight vineyards in England, with Ely marking the most northerly spot, seventy miles northeast of London. It was a warmer world. Archaeological evidence indicates that the years 950 to 1300 were marked by noticeably warmer temperatures than we experience today, even in the age of "global warming." Meteorologists describe this medieval warm epoch as the "Little Optimum," and they cite it as the explanation of such phenomena as the Viking explosion into Russia, France, Iceland, and the northwestern Atlantic.

The northerly retreat of icebergs and pack-ice under the impact of warmer temperatures is a plausible explanation of why Lief Eriksson was able to sail round the top of the Atlantic as far as Newfoundland in or about the year 1000, and why he found vines there. During the "Little Optimum," Edinburgh enjoyed the climate of London, while London enjoyed the climate of the Loire valley in France, a difference of 2 to 4 degrees Fahrenheit — the equivalent in modern American terms of San Francisco's climate moving north to Seattle.[101]

Weather was a subject of intense interest to the Anglo-Saxons, and with their seafaring heritage they reckoned they understood it well.

"If the sky reddens at night," wrote the Venerable Bede, "[it foretells] a clear day; if in the morning, it means bad weather. . . . Also, when during a night voyage, the sea glitters about the oars, there will be a storm. And when dolphins often leap above the water, by what they say, there will result a wind rising, and breaking clouds will open the heavens."[102]

One ninth-century manuscript was dedicated exclusively to thunder and what it might mean: "In May, thunder presages a hungry year. . . . In the month of July, thunder signifies crops turning out well, and livestock perishing. . . . If it thunders on Sunday, this is considered to presage an extensive mortality of monks and nuns. . . . Of thunder on Wednesday, there is no doubt that it presages the death of idle and scandalous prostitutes."[103]

The modern reader has to wonder what went through the mind of the monk or the nun who was reading these predictions and who recalled, say, the last time they heard a fierce clap of thunder on a Sunday, but saw none of their colleagues dropping down dead. Auguries have an eternal fascination, and for those who take them seriously, it never seems to matter if cold reality proves them wrong. In the year 1000 people gave the benefit of the doubt to the intangible aspects of their life. It was an acknowledgement that they did not know all the answers, and it also served, perhaps, as an insurance policy in the event that the facts on which they were relying proved faulty.

King Alfred took no chances. The *Anglo-Saxon Chronicle*

gave the great king an impressive genealogy which traced his ancestry back from the ninth century to Noah and thence, via Methusaleh and other Old Testament figures, back to Adam — "the first man and our father who is Christ. Amen."[104] But the king's family tree also showed that he claimed descent from one of the greatest of the Germanic gods, Woden, master magician, calmer of storms, raiser of the dead and governor of victory,[105] with another section of the royal genealogy featuring such figures as the mythical *Beow* or Barley, the basis for the folk figure John Barleycorn, who was an ancient pagan focus for rituals of sacrifice.

The old gods still stalked the furrows of Anglo-Saxon England. The word pagan comes from *pagus*, Latin for "the countryside," and it was among the "pags," or the rustics, that the old magic lived on. When the ploughman went out to cut his first furrow in January or February, you might have seen him say a prayer as he knelt to scoop a shallow nest in the soil for a cake that his wife had baked:

> *Earth, Earth, Earth! Oh Earth our mother!*
> *May the all-wielder, Ever-Lord grant thee*
> *Acres a-waxing, upwards a-growing,*
> *Pregnant with corn and plenteous in strength.*[106]

The cake was baked from the same grain that the farmer was hoping to cultivate, and Bede related how February was popularly known as "the month of cakes," after the cakes or *placentae* "which in that month the English offered to their gods."[107]

Bede and the other monkish chroniclers were not inclined to celebrate England's heathen heritage. You have to comb their writings carefully for clues to paganism. But even in their Christian loyalties they conveyed a live-and-let-live impression of the relations between England's old and new religions:

> I cannot abandon the age-old beliefs that I have held. . . . [declared Ethelbert, the last pagan king of Kent, according to Bede's history, as he addressed Augustine and his fellow Christian missionaries in 597]. But since you have travelled far, and I can see that you are sincere in your desire to impart to us what you believe to be true and excellent, we will not harm you. . . . Nor will we forbid you to preach and win any people you can to your religion.[108]

Bede went on to describe how King Ethelbert had provided the Christian missionaries with a base inside Canterbury, and how Pope Gregory, sending instructions from Rome, exhibited parallel tolerance:

> You are familiar with the usage of the Roman church . . . [the Pope told Augustine]. But if you have found customs, whether in the church of Rome or of Gaul or any other that may be more acceptable to God, I wish you to make a careful selection of them. . . . For in these days the church corrects some things strictly, and allows others out of leniency. Others again she deliberately glosses over and tolerates, and by doing so often succeeds in checking an evil of which she disapproves.

Gregory suggested to Augustine that England's old pagan temples should be turned into Christian churches "in order that the people may the more familiarly resort to the places to which they have been accustomed," and, as a result, there are modern English churches which can be traced back to the site of Bronze Age barrows. Rather than sacrifice to Mother Earth, Anglo-Saxons were encouraged to direct their prayers to the Virgin Mary, and having accepted Sunday and Moon-day, the church also tolerated Tiw's-day, Woden's-day, Thor's-day, and Frig's-day, the English days of the week that were named after the old Norse gods Tiw, the god of war, Woden, Alfred's father of the gods and of the royal house of Wessex, Thunor, the god of thunder, and Frig, the goddess of growing things and fertility. Saturn's day was another pagan hangover — from the Romans.

King Aldwulf of East Anglia, who was a contemporary of Bede's, recalled how he had seen in his boyhood the temple created by his predecessor King Redwald, who wanted to keep in favour with both religions and had had two altars constructed side by side. At one altar the king partook of bread and wine, "the holy sacrifice of Christ," while at the other he sacrificed in the old style.[109] Bede made it very clear that this must be considered an ignoble and ignorant attempt to serve two masters, but his description of why King Ethelbert eventually decided to become Christian was couched in bloodlessly pragmatic terms. According to Bede, the king of Kent did not switch to the new religion through any deeply personal or emotion-led revelation, but simply because he came to judge that the new belief system offered better prospects for him and for his kingdom than the old.

New magic for old was the language of conversion. The plain-talking Boniface made his mark in Germany when he cut down a sacred grove of trees and used the wood to build a new church for Jesus. The local shamans predicted disaster, but lightning did not strike, and Boniface was soon presiding over mass conversions. The beautiful fourteen-foot-high stone cross that stands at Gosforth in Cumbria is carved with a panoply of Norse gods, with the evil god Loki chained beneath a venomous serpent, while Woden fights off a wolf amidst a cluster of dragons — and the figure of Christ looms crucified at the apex of the battle, not so much the only god as the most powerful one.

The millennium saw a rush of European regimes anxious to join the Christian club, from Vladimir of Kiev, King of the Rus, who was baptised in 988, to the Viking assembly of Iceland and King Stephen of Hungary, both converts in the year 1000 itself. As these societies around the geographical margin signed up for inclusion in the belief system of the European core, one is tempted to see a modern parallel with the nations of Europe's fringe, all standing in line to join the European Economic Community at the end of the second millennium. To be Christian was to be modern in the year 1000, the token of a society's eagerness for centralised authority, an organised coinage and taxation system, and, above all, a cohesive national identity that was energetically preached and sanctified by the church. When Canute established himself in England in 1016, he set up his Danish court in Winchester, where, in a series of ceremonies in the great cathedral that were carefully publicised by the religious chroniclers, he used Christianity to sanctify his new power and authority.

Canute's decision to run his North Sea empire from England, and not from Scandinavia, was a tribute to the cultural and political status that the country had achieved by the beginning of the eleventh century, but it was also a tribute to England's religion. In the battle between paganism and Christianity, Christianity had come out on top, and in quite a rush. The cavalcade of Christian conversions in the final years of the century has another modern parallel: after decades of bitter and tense conflict between two mighty ideologies, one had collapsed as the millennium approached, leaving the other in charge of the agenda with a conclusiveness that had long been preached with fervour, but which had not been that obvious when the battle was at its height.

OCTOBER

WAR GAMES

THE WAVY LINE WHICH MARKS THE BACK-ground to this calendar drawing for October invites us to contemplate a range of hills, from whose heights descends a tumbling river. As the river reaches the foreground, it turns into a lake on which two waterfowl splash happily, unaware that they are sitting targets for the falcons on the huntsmen's wrists. It is an ambitious picture, in which landscape, the threat of death, and the atmosphere of a late autumn afternoon's hunting are all packed tightly into a few lines sketched on a sheet of parchment, and the exaggerated size of the lumbering bird in the foreground might suggest that the artist has made some error of perspective. But the drawing of the bird is quite accurate, for a thousand years ago England's wildlife was more exotic than it is today. Our huntsmen's quarry is the huge European crane, a common sight in England until it was hunted to extinction sometime in the sixteenth century.[110]

Hunting in the year 1000 was still a democratic pastime. Every free-born Anglo-Saxon had the right to enter the forest and bring home game for the pot. But these well-dressed huntsmen have a rich air about them — and their horse is equally well dressed. The hunting restrictions which the Normans introduced after 1066 were one of the principal sources of friction between the native population and the new regime, and the fat horseman with his friend the falconer prefigure that social conflict. The power, magic, and pleasures of full-scale hunting were stolen by the upper crust, and it was in the eleventh century that the peculiarly English connotations of hunting as a class-sensitive activity became attached to the country pursuit that is still enjoyed in most other societies by "haves" and "have-nots" alike.

Medieval hunting was both a metaphor and a preparation for war. It kept horse and rider fit, and, more significantly, it fostered the camaraderie of the warrior band. It was like a training session. The lord and his retainers went out hunting together to network, plot, and rehearse future acquisitions as the twentieth-century corporate raider sets up deals over golf. Between 950 and 1066 England was the most fought-over kingdom in western Europe. Its merchants were trading and its farmers were producing the food that was needed to sustain an expanding population. But this very prosperity made the country prey to leaner, tougher predators. Forget Merrie England. Think gangland Chicago in the 1930s, or the drug gangs of south Los Angeles today.

Power politics in the year 1000 can best be understood by observing how gangs and Mafias operate. Though frightening to outsiders, the structure of the gang offers cohesion, protection, and a sense of belonging to its "family." Its hierarchy is both intimidating and reassuring, and while the leader may operate on the basis of fear, he scares his followers less than the alternatives in a lawless and chaotic environment. The successful Godfather also provides the weak and needy with a form of welfare in exchange for their loyalty — or "fealty" as it was called in the year 1000. The mark of King Athelstan's authority was an oath of allegiance sworn by every boy in tenth-century Engla-lond (slaves excepted) when they reached the age of twelve: "In the first place, all shall swear in the name of the Lord, before whom every holy thing is holy, that they will be faithful to the king."

The fact that this oath was administered by the local sheriff, who rode round the countryside as the embodiment of law and order, conjures up comparisons with the American Wild West — another embryonic society that was anxious to strengthen its fragile laws and to curb the powers of the lawless and over-mighty. In the year 1000, it was the job of the king's shire reeve to visit every community at least once a year and to administer the oath in a ceremony whose religious content was significant. The sheriff's visit frequently took place in October after the harvest had been gathered in, and one can imagine the boys of the village apprehensively assembled for their first taste of adult responsibility.

"Even as it behoves a man to be faithful to his lord," ran the royal instruction, "without dispute or dissention, openly or in secret, favouring what the lord favours and discountenancing what he discountenances, so, from the day on which this oath shall be rendered, no one shall conceal the breach of it on the part of a brother or family relation, any more than in a stranger."

This was the key promise, for it made it your duty as a loyal member of your community to turn in anyone who was not behaving himself — Guardian Angels meet Neighbourhood Watch.

This oath, later known as the "frank pledge," was part of tenth-century England's increasingly organised system of government, by which the shires were subdivided into "hundreds" — groupings of a hundred households, more or less. These hundreds were subdivided in turn into the smaller, local "frank pledge" groups of roughly ten or a dozen households, in which each member was held accountable for the good conduct of his fellows. The essence of the frank pledge system was that it transformed obeying the rules from a matter of impersonal obedience into personal loyalty, which was then extended up the ladder in a series of easily comprehensible steps to the principal lord, whose authority was endorsed by God.

In the Danelaw of northeastern England, the hundreds were generally known as "wapentakes" from the Old Norse *vapnatak*, meaning just what it sounds, "weapon-taking," since this was what loyalty and government all boiled down to in the year 1000 — the rounding up of men and weapons. It is the unmentionable reality of civilisation that it depends on fighting. All the great societies have been based on military success, and in the final analysis, the Anglo-Saxon king was the leader of the war band.

It was as military leader that the king had most need to play the part of the ruthless gang boss, since his principal lieutenants were all gangsters themselves. That was their qualification for the job. The greatest lords were the greatest thugs, for the English aristocracy, like the military elite of every European country in the year 1000, was a cadre that had been trained to kill. To be noble was to wear a sword and throw your weight around, and in 1012, the pious Alphege, archbishop of Canterbury, discovered to his cost what could happen when the war dogs got drunk.

The archbishop had been captured by the Danes the previous year and had been held hostage in conditions of apparent civility. He had got close enough to his captors to convert and baptise at least one of them, until one night at Greenwich when the assembled crowd of noblemen, the cream of the Danish king's generals and courtiers, got started on a consignment of wine which had arrived "from the south" and which evidently called for special celebration. The evening's fun culminated with the Danish aristocracy pelting the unfortunate archbishop with a hail of cattle bones and skulls from the beef on which they had been feasting. Alphege bore up valiantly under this savage horseplay, until he was struck by one blow too many and fell on the floor bleeding — finally succumbing when his skull was crushed by the blunt end of a battle-axe wielded by the very nobleman whom he had converted and blessed the previous day.

These were the ruffians who were idealised by the poems of the time. The warrior was a hero, and the comradely ethos of the warrior fraternity provided the running theme for epic sagas like *Beowulf* and *The Battle of Maldon*. This was no Camelot. The chivalry of King Arthur and his Knights of the Round Table was a fable developed a century and a half later, based on the possible existence of a British chieftain named Arthur who fought in the dark confusion which followed the departure of the Romans, and it is unlikely that the sixth-century Arthur operated on any particularly chivalrous basis.

The fundamental rule of warfare in the year 1000 was to avoid battle wherever possible. Whole summers could be occupied by armies manoeuvring to avoid each other. The basic mistake of the white-haired Byrhtnoth at the Battle of Maldon had been to seek confrontation. Battle in the first millennium was rather like a deadly rugby scrum — with both sides wearing the same colour shirts. There were none of the distinguishing liveries and coats of arms developed in later centuries, and in the confused melée the warrior probably distinguished friend from foe by looking into their faces. Armies were small — a few thousand men constituted an exceptionally large host — so that most protagonists would have known their own side by sight. In this comparatively intimate environment, you stood less chance of being killed than in modern mechanised warfare, but to be wounded was a more serious matter, since the smallest wounds could prove fatal in the absence of proper medical care.

In the front line stood the youngest, strongest, and most expendable warriors, forming a defensive row with their shields held chest high in front of them, touching or overlapping. Their spears protruded from the chinks in this formation that was known as the "shieldwall" or "war hedge." Behind this front rank were ranged the more lightly armed and mobile second rank, whose job was to plug holes in the shieldwall and act as liaison between the front line and headquarters that lay straight behind them. This was the leader, armed and armoured like the rest of his men, on foot and surrounded by his own personal bodyguard, the "house-carls" or hearth companions who made up his personal retinue. In times of peace, the king's hearth companions were the nearest equivalent to a police force: they administered his laws and enforced his royal authority.

The tactics of engagement were almost ritual. The two sides drew up their forces in opposing "shieldwall" rows, taking advantage of any geographical features such as water or woods to protect their flank. In the case of Harold and the English on 14 October 1066, they occupied the high ground on Caldbeck Hill to the west of Hastings, as the Normans advanced across the saltmarshes and struck inland from the sea.

Hostilities opened with a mutual throwing of spears and a random loosing of arrows, probably accompanied by loud jeering and shouting to get the blood up. English soldiers handled sturdy bows of yew, ash, or elm, which could propel an iron-tipped arrow as far as a hundred yards: excavations have uncovered English arrows with personal markings which suggest that bowmen tried to retrieve their arrows after a battle, since each beaten iron arrow tip represented quite an investment.

The Anglo-Saxon foot soldier also brought his own throwing spears to the field, along with his sword and shield. He was an all-purpose, multifunction warrior, and the Anglo-Saxon army was the last army in western Europe to fight as one homogeneous host. It was not divided into separate divisions of cavalry, infantry, and bowmen — unlike the Normans — and this was one of the reasons why the Normans won at Hastings and the Anglo-Saxons lost.

Our best evidence of what an Anglo-Saxon army looked like comes from the Bayeux tapestry, stitched in celebration of the victory sometime in the next sixteen years or so — not in Bayeux, but most probably in Canterbury by English embroiderers working to the commission of William the Conqueror's kinsman Odo, bishop of Bayeux. The tapestry shows King Harold's house carls wielding their formidable battle-axes, but most of the English are armed and dressed exactly like their Norman foes, wearing suits of ringed mail from head to knee and pointed helmets that feature a protective bridge of metal jutting downwards to shield the nose. Today this heavy, nose-guarded helmet is the distinguishing mark of wicked Norman soldiers in Robin Hood movies, but in the years around 1000 the nose-guarded helmet was, in fact, worn by Saxon, Viking, and Norman alike.

The major and decisive distinction which the Bayeux tapestry does make clear about the two sides at the Battle of Hastings is that the Normans rode horses, while the English fought on foot. From the time of King Alfred, if not earlier, the English army would ride horses in order to reach the battlefield — but once at the field, those horses would be led away. The animals played no part in combat, but were kept tethered nearby, ready to hasten a speedy withdrawal or, more hopefully, to assist in the pursuit of a fleeing foe.

The first time that an English army ever faced mounted cavalry was in 1066, and accounts of the battle of Hastings suggest that the shieldwall initially held up well against the charges of the Norman knights on their *destriers* — the muscular and nimble chargers, specially bred for battle, which made the Normans the most formidable fighting force in Europe. Two rival military technologies battled for control of the rich and sophisticated civilisation of Anglo-Saxon England on that October Saturday in 1066, and the new technology won. Tired by the successful northern campaign they had just fought, travelling up to Stamford Bridge to repel the invading army of the Norwegian Harald Hardrade, the English foot soldiers were ground down by the Norman cavalry as the afternoon wore on.

A mile away, nobody heard a thing. Without gunfire or explosions, early medieval battles were a series of muffled confrontations enlivened only by the metallic clash of sword on sword and by the war cries — *"Dex Aie"* ("God's help") from the Norman side and "Out! Out!" from the English as they repulsed attackers from their shieldwall, probably uttering their call in what we would consider a North Country accent.[111]

Both Harald Hardrade and William of Normandy had landed in England in the autumn month when war was most popular in the years around 1000. No army went campaigning in the winter if it could help it, and during the summer every able-bodied man had work to do on the land. By October, however, your soldiers had finished gathering in the harvest, while the countryside was dotted with barns full of grain — the ideal moment for raiding. From the farmer's point of view, a particular hazard of being raided and having your storerooms ravaged straight after the harvest was that you could not only starve through the winter, you would lose your stock of seed corn as well. One serious autumn raid could mean ruin for generations to come.

It is hardly surprising that so many sports and pastimes related to war in the year 1000. Riding and archery had obvious practical applications, while the strategies of the chessboard provided a metaphor for the manoeuvrings of the battlefield. Developed in the East, chess reached Spain and southern France thanks to the Arabs. It is not certain when it arrived in England, but a Swiss poem of the 990s describes the moves of the queen and how the game ends when the king is in check-mate. In the year 1000 the queen was actually one of the weaker pieces on the board, and the game was even slower and more long-drawn-out than it is today. It was not until the fifteenth century that the queen was given the extraordinary range of moves which made her the superpower of the board, when the game was so revolutionised that it was sometimes renamed New Chess, Queen's Chess, or La Dame Enragée.

There were no playing cards in the year 1000. They did not appear in Europe until the fourteenth century. But we have evidence of people playing backgammon as well as noughts and crosses [ticktacktoe]. With the nights getting longer, the Anglo-Saxons stretched their ability to keep themselves amused, and they derived particular fun from riddles which were often quite poetic — as their poems could be riddle-like:

> Multicoloured in hue, I flee the sky and the deep earth.
> There is no place for me on the ground, nor in any part
>   of the poles.
> No one fears an exile as cruel as mine,
> But I make the world grow green with my rainy tears.

The answer to this puzzle, composed by the seventh-century scholar St. Aldhelm, was "a cloud." Beloved of King Alfred, Aldhelm's verses were sung with harp accompaniment to draw people into church, and his riddles survive in a tenth-century manuscript in the library of Canterbury Cathedral.

Down in Exeter, a still more comprehensive collection of riddles survives in the Cathedral Library — the *Exeter Book*, an eleventh-century volume whose much-scarred cover seems to have done service as a cutting board for bread and cheese. To judge from the brown ring-like stains on its first folio, it was also used as a beer mat, and some of its riddles have a quality to match:

> *I am a strange creature, for I satisfy women . . .*
> *I grow very tall, erect in a bed,*
> *I'm hairy underneath. From time to time*
> *A beautiful girl, the brave daughter*
> *Of some fellow dares to hold me*
> *Grips my reddish skin, robs me of my head*
> *And puts me in the pantry. At once that girl*
> *With plaited hair who has confined me*
> *Remembers our meeting. Her eye moistens.*[112]

The answer? An onion. What other answer could there be? The riddle for a milk churn delighted in similar double entendre:

> *A man came walking where he knew*
> *She stood in a corner, stepped forward;*
> *The bold fellow plucked up his own*
> *Skirt by hand, stuck something stiff*
> *Beneath her belt as she stood,*
> *Worked his will. They both wiggled.*
> *The man hurried: his trusty helper*
> *Plied a handy task, but tired*
> *At length, less strong now than she,*
> *Weary of the work. Thick beneath*

Her belt swelled the thing good men
Praise with their hearts and purses.[113]

These earthy tenth-century jokes were copied onto parchment by monks in their finest hand, and they show that the Anglo-Saxon male had a lusty sense of humour. But what do we know about how the women felt?

NOVEMBER

FEMALES AND THE
PRICE OF FONDLING

W E HAVE REACHED NOVEMBER —
nearly the end of the year — and there has
not been a single drawing in the Julius Work
Calendar that shows women working, playing, or fulfilling
any role, trivial or important, in the life of Engla-lond in the
years around 1000. Nor will December remedy the matter,
since, like every other document that has come down to us
from those times, the Julius Work Calendar was the work
of male sensibilities operating in a world where language
and the structures of thought itself were framed in unquestioningly male terms.

The Old English for a human being was *mann*. All human beings were *menn*, the term being used for both sexes,
in the same way that women are today supposed to be
included in the meaning of such words as "mankind." One
eleventh-century document talks of the descendants of
Adam and Eve as "descended from two men," and while this
displayed a mental framework that may strike us today as
gender-insensitive, it also contained a certain assumption of
male-female equality. One charter of 969 A.D. discussed
land near Worcester that had been held by a man called

Elfweard: "Elfweard was the first man . . ." ran the document. "Now it is in the hands of his daughter, and she is the second man."[114] Thirty wills survive today from the late Anglo-Saxon period and ten of those are the wills of women, each of whom was a significant property owner, with the same rights of ownership and bequeathal as any man. In the year 1000 the role that women played in English society was more complex than surface impressions might suggest.

The reign of King Ethelred took its character from two powerful women. It could even be argued that the women were more powerful than Ethelred himself, who came to the throne as a boy aged only ten or twelve, thanks to the mysterious murder of his half brother Edward at Corfe in Dorset in 978 A.D. No one was ever punished for the violence, but it has generally been presumed that his death had something to do with Ethelred's mother, the dowager queen Aelfthryth, who thus secured the throne for her own blood line, along with power for herself as regent. The church at the time drew a veil over the ugly incident, since the dead Edward's reign had been marked by notable hostility towards the recently refounded monasteries, in notable contrast to Aelfthryth, who made herself the leading patron of church reform. So in the year 1000, both the king of England and the reforming church hierarchy owed their power to the ambition of the same dynamic woman.

In 1002 Ethelred, now in his early thirties, tried to bolster his wavering authority by marrying Emma, the sister of Duke Richard II of Normandy. It must have been an intimidating moment for the young woman when she crossed the Channel from France that spring to meet Ethelred, who had already fathered six sons, and at least four daughters, by previous liaisons. Only just a teenager, and perhaps as young as twelve, Emma spoke no English, and was required by her new husband to take the *Englisc* name of Aelfgifu. This alliance of convenience was a classic example of the Anglo-Saxon concept of the female "peace-weaver" — the woman whose feminine qualities were supposed to weave new bonds of family loyalty.

But Emma was to prove a personality in her own right. Before she was twenty her strength of character had made her one of the most powerful figures in Ethelred's circle, and after Ethelred's death his Danish successor Canute sidelined his first wife to marry her. Emma's stature provided the authority that the foreign king knew that he needed. After Canute died he was briefly succeeded by Harold Harefoot, his son by his first marriage, but after Harefoot's death, it was Emma's blood that took over, first in the shape of Harthacanute, her son by Canute, and then by the son she had borne Ethelred, the half-English, half-Norman Edward the Confessor, whose links with his blood relation William of Normandy paved the way for the Anglo-Norman polity. Emma had been married to two kings of Engla-lond, and she was the mother of two more.

Anglo-Saxon kings did not succeed on the basis of primogeniture. All the king's offspring were known as aethelings — throneworthy — and from this gene pool the royal family would select the aetheling who seemed best qualified for the job. It was the practical way to maintain the wealth and preeminence of the ruling clan. King Alfred

was a youngest brother who became king of Wessex in pref-
erence to sons of his elder siblings, while in Ireland an
extended version of the same principle circulated sover-
eignty around different clans on a rota basis. It was comparable to the selection by family consensus that is operated
by Bedouin Arab monarchies today. In England the system
produced a variegated succession of monarchs who were
generally more capable than those thrown up by a rigid line
of inheritance — and it also offered power to those royal
mothers who succeeded in raising competent and forceful
sons. Operating through the male line, the women had the
chance to make themselves the key.

Nepotism was nothing to be ashamed of in the years
around 1000. It was the purpose of family existence. The
mother who advanced her clan's power earned the respect
of the entire community, and it is significant that this era
saw the beginning in England of the cult of the Virgin
Mary, the mother who raised the most powerful son of all.
A tenth-century collection of blessings written for Bishop
Ethelwold contains one of the first representations of Mary
being crowned that survives in the West. The Virgin is
shown not as a carpenter's wife, which would have made her
very easily identifiable with most of the people who prayed
to her, but as a worldly queen, wearing a crown. It was
another aspect of the developing alliance between crown
and church, and the image was the more significant for
being propagated by a church which had found natural
allies in tough royal matrons like Aelfthryth and Emma. At
the end of her life, Emma refused to follow tradition and
retire to a nunnery, but stayed active in dynastic politics.
She commissioned her own biography to make sure that

her life was remembered as she wished to be — and she is remembered as Emma, not Aelfgifu.

To judge from the *Anglo-Saxon Chronicle*, the most dynamic royal matron of the tenth century was Alfred's daughter Aethelflaed, who took up the English campaign against the Danes after her father's death, in alliance with her brother Edward, earning herself the title "Lady of the Mercians." Aethelflaed was married to the monarch of the Midland kingdom of Mercia, but she ran the country herself for seven years after his death, pursuing her father's policy of building fortified *burhs* against the Danes — and leading her soldiers in a personal capacity, according to the *Chronicle* entry from 913:

> In this year, by the grace of God, Aethelflaed, Lady of the Mercians, went with all the Mercians to Tamworth, and built the fortress there in early summer and before the beginning of August, the one at Stafford.[115]

In 916 Aethelflaed sent a punitive expedition against some Welsh invaders, then turned her attention to the Vikings, from whom she won back the *burhs* of Derby and Leicester. "She protected her own men and terrified aliens," wrote William of Malmesbury, a post-Conquest historian who seemed more surprised than were the Anglo-Saxon chroniclers that a woman should achieve so much. Starting her programme of fortress building in 910 A.D., Aethelflaed got ten *burhs* completed in less than five years, and led her Mercians to victories that made her one of the most powerful figures in early tenth-century England. We can imagine this latter-day Boadicea standing behind the shieldwall, inspiring the loyalty of her own troops and winning the awed respect of her enemies. By 918 the Vikings in York had volunteered their allegiance to Aethelflaed without a fight. Alongside her father, Alfred, the Lady of the Mercians was one of England's folk heroes in the year 1000, remembered and respected as a tough woman in tough times, and her reputation was to grow with the retelling.

Another female category of *mann* who had no option but to be tough were the women who ran the monasteries of early Anglo-Saxon England. Some fifty of the religious communities founded in the seventh century were double houses, where men and women lived and worshipped side by side, and the records indicate that all of these double houses were under the direction of a female. Everyone answered to the abbess, not the abbot.[116] It was evidently not a problem for a community of educated men to submit to the authority of a woman thirteen hundred years ago, though the documents do show that the abbesses in charge of double houses were all aethelings — members of royal families. Among these pioneering female missionaries the most famous was the abbess Hilda, who founded (or possibly refounded) the abbey of Whitby on the Yorkshire coast, where in 664 she hosted the famous Synod of Whitby, at which Celtic and Rome-supporting Christians met to argue over the date of Easter.

"All who knew her," wrote the Venerable Bede, "called her 'mother.'"[117]

It was under Hilda's encouragement that the Whitby cowherd Caedmon produced the first Christian poems and songs in English, and Hilda got her monks to learn and propagate the poet's evangelising songs. According to Bede, she also "compelled those under her direction to devote time to the study of the holy scriptures" with such success that no less than five of her monkish pupils went on to become bishops.[118] Within a few years of her death in 680 A.D. Hilda was being hailed as a saint, and to this day pious tradition has it that the migrating geese who fly down from the Arctic to rest on the headland near the site of Whitby's old abbey are pilgrims paying homage to her memory. By the year 1000 there were at least fifteen English churches dedicated to St. Hilda, where her feast was celebrated every year on November 17.

By the year 1000, however, the sacred Hilda and the pioneering double monasteries run by royal women were a three-hundred-year-old memory. Of the new religious houses founded in the tenth century, some thirty were monasteries, and only half a dozen were nunneries. There were no double houses and the brother-sister relationships of Hilda's day had been replaced by a more rigid segregation. The church was tightening up on matters sexual. Until the middle of the tenth century it had been quite routine for priests to be married. The records show that in the early 960s the cathedral at Winchester was administered by a group of canons, every one of whom was married. But Dunstan, Ethelwold, and the new church reformers disapproved of this. Celibacy was the way ahead for the modern canon, and Ethelwold fiercely confronted the happy husbands of Winchester in 964 A.D. He gave them the choice between their wives and their jobs, and when they all chose their wives, they were drummed out of the cathedral to be replaced by a team of celibate monks from Abingdon.

One cannot imagine the pious bishop Ethelwold deriving much amusement from riddles about hairy onions or the pleasures of vigorous butter churning. The buildup to the millennium saw a new element of puritanical asceticism claiming control of religion — the Nanny Church. The censorious Ethelwold took it upon himself to rebuke young St. Edith of Wilton for a style of dress which he considered too grand. "Christ," he said, "asked for the heart."

"Quite so, Father," responded Edith. "And I have given my heart."[119]

Edith, who died aged only twenty-two after a blameless life, may have felt able to stand up to the old priest because she was a king's daughter, albeit the product of King Edgar's union with Wulfrida, his Kentish mistress. By the end of the tenth century, Edith's humility had inspired a cult of holy wells in Kent, Staffordshire, and Herefordshire. Their waters were deemed efficacious for eye conditions.

Generally, the church met no resistance as it claimed more control of everyday life — and as it sought, in particular, to shape the marriage arrangements which it had hitherto been content to leave to local custom. Anglo-Saxon weddings were traditional folk ceremonies which went back to pagan times. A couple might stop at the church porch for a blessing from the priest, but the essence of the ceremony was the ritual of secular toasts, vows, and speeches enjoyed with the rest of the village. Such a secular bonding could also be broken in a secular fashion, and though the records are scanty, thanks to filtering by the church in later years, it does seem that Anglo-Saxons separated and divorced when they had to, without any particular ethical complications. The only concern of the community was practical — the proper partitioning of property and the care of the children. One Anglo-Saxon law code makes clear that a woman could walk out of her marriage on her own initiative if she cared to, and that if she took the children and cared for them, then she was also entitled to half the property.[120]

The Old English law codes were concerned to shield women against the hazards of life in a rough, male-dominated society. If the epic poetry of the time embodied the aggressive male ethos of the warrior band, the law codes stood for the opposing rights of the physically frailer sex. This might seem an unlikely consequence of a lawmaking process that flowed through the confabulations of male monarchs with their male advisers, but it directly reflected the values enshrined in the language of *Englisc*: men were called *waepnedmenn*, "weaponed-persons," while women were *wifmenn*, "wife-persons," with *wif* being derived from the word for "weaving." In a world where order was uncertain and shops virtually nonexistent, the man's job was to provide protection, while the woman provided clothes, and this division of responsibility was reflected in the grave goods with which pagan Anglo-Saxons were buried: male skeletons are found with their swords, spears, and shields; women are buried with spindles, weaving batons, and small, symbolic sewing boxes that contain needles, thread, and even minute samples of cloth.

By the year 1000 people were no longer being buried in this fashion. The church told believers that they had no need of physical adornment or accessories for the next world. The church way was taking hold, and a moralistic tone was entering the legal equation. "If a woman during her husband's life commits adultery with another man . . ." read Law 53 of Canute, "her legal husband is to have all her property, and she is to lose her nose and her ears."[121]

This gruesome regulation — which enjoined no similar penalty for the male adulterer — proved short-lived. It died with Canute in 1035. The only other English law ever to treat adultery so brutally was passed six hundred years later as part of Oliver Cromwell's attempt to make England godly. The underlying legal principles of Anglo-Saxon life were essentially uncensorious. Every man — and woman — had their price, the so-called *wergild*, and even morally loaded offences were regulated according to its pragmatic terms: "If a freeman lie with a freeman's wife," read one code of Kentish law, "let him pay for it with her *wergild*, and provide another wife out of his own money."[122]

This money-based attitude to public morals was applied remorselessly down the social scale. If a man lay with a virgin who was a slave in the royal household, he owed compensation of fifty shillings; if she was one of the slaves working in the royal flour mill, the compensation was twenty-five shillings — and if she was of the lowest class of slave, the payment was twelve shillings.[123]

At the end of the ninth century, the enlightened King Alfred worked on the same principle when it came to sexual harassment: a man who fondled the breast of a freewoman, uninvited, incurred a fine of five shillings, while throwing the woman down, though not actually violating her, cost ten shillings. Rape was six times more serious. The violation of a freewoman demanded compensation of sixty shillings — payable, like all the other fines, directly to her.

This was another principle of Anglo-Saxon law that had become established by the year 1000. Marriage law was essentially about the allocation of property, and marriage contracts usually involved negotiations between male heads of households over the *morgengifu*, literally the morning gift, paid over by the husband after the satisfactory completion of the wedding night. But the payment, which could involve substantial amounts of money and land, went to the woman herself, which gave a girl a solid financial interest in maintaining her virginity until marriage.

The laws did not specifically require that the bride should be a virgin. If the husband had no complaint, the law saw no need to get involved. But King Aethelbert did provide that the morning gift should be repaid by the wife in cases of deception, thus protecting the bridegroom who had paid out his morning gift for a woman who turned out to be carrying another man's child,[124] while one of Alfred's laws made a certain allowance for crimes of passion: a man who found "another man with his wedded wife, within closed doors or under the same blanket; or if he finds another man with his legitimate daughter or sister or with his mother, if she has been given in wedlock to his father, can fight the intruder with impunity. If he kills the man, his kin will not be allowed to avenge him."[125]

There is a stocky, matter-of-fact tone to these Anglo-Saxon laws. From the earliest date the principle was clearly established that a woman could not be held responsible for the criminal activity of her husband — though she was judged as guilty as he if the facts proved that she had been his accomplice: "If anyone shall steal in such a way that his wife and children know nothing of it," ran the seventh-century law of King Ine of Wessex, "he shall pay sixty shillings as fine. But if he steals with the knowledge of all his household, they are all to go into slavery." Four hundred years later Canute refined the principle: a woman could not be held guilty for her husband's theft, he decreed, unless the stolen property was found in one of the specific places for which, as keeper of the household keys, she was responsible — the house's storeroom, any large chest, or any small chest of the sort used to store jewellery.[126]

The calendar drawing for the month of November could possibly depict the grisly penalty inflicted on those who were suspected of theft. It shows a figure heating an iron in the fire, and the obvious presumption might be that he is a blacksmith forging something like a horseshoe. This interpretation, however, makes no sense of the surrounding figures in the picture, who are better explained by another scenario.

To the left of the picture stands a neat pile of carefully cured and planed wooden planks and it could well be that the figure beside them, captured by the artist in the act of bearing away a stack of wood, is up to no good. He is suspected of being a thief, and as such he is brought to the ordeal by the two ceremonially clothed agents of justice on the right of the drawing, one of whom is carrying a rolled legal scroll. The suspect is now barefoot, and he holds his hands up ready for the ghastly test. He will be required to grasp the red-hot iron and step out nine paces, after which his wounds will be dressed and kept covered for a week. If, when the bandages are unbound, his wounds clearly appear to be healing, he will be judged not guilty. But if the wounds have gone septic, which could well be the death of him in any case, he will suffer the penalty for theft in the year 1000 — hanging until dead.

The gallows stood outside every medieval town and at rural crossroads, displaying its grisly cargo, which would twist in the wind until the birds picked the bones clean. It was not a pretty sight, and it was not intended to be. Along with trial by ordeal, hanging was the most effective deterrent that could be devised in an age without police or prisons. Don't mess with justice, ran the message. It is not worth the risk.

The risk was severe for those who could not buy their way out of trouble. The *wergild* system meant that the rich could pay for their transgressions at the rate of 125 pounds of silver for each human life. So while a murderous nobleman could avoid the death penalty by paying for the life he had taken, it was most unlikely that a thief had the funds to make any sort of restitution. Whether women were hanged just like men, we do not know. But it seems likely that this was one aspect of life and death in the year 1000 to which sexual equality did apply.

DECEMBER

THE END OF THINGS,
OR A NEW BEGINNING?

Then I saw an angel coming down from heaven with the key of the abyss and a great chain in his hands. He seized the dragon, that serpent of old, the Devil or Satan, and chained him up for a thousand years; he threw him into the abyss, shutting and sealing it over him, so that he might seduce the nations no more till the thousand years were over. After that he must be let loose for a short while.

— *Revelation 20:1-3*

THERE WERE NO SUCH THINGS AS GOSSIP columnists in the year 1000, but if *Vanity Fair* had existed, it would certainly have found room for the writings of Ralph Glaber. Glaber was a Burgundian monk who wrote a five-volume history of his times which constitutes our principal surviving source as to how people might have felt in the year 1000 about the shift in the calendar from one millennium to the next. Computer anxieties aside, most people today are looking forward to 2000 and the years beyond with reasonable optimism. But a thousand years ago people had never lived through such a major milestone, and biblical passages like the Revelation of St. John proposed unpleasant possibilities. Would the world come to an end? Would there be another millennium? Would life continue, but in some less pleasant form, reflecting the unchaining of Satan that St. John had described?

Ralph Glaber wrote his history with these questions in mind. He entered his first monastery in 997 A.D. Scarcely a dozen years old, he seems to have been possessed of a troublemaking character which set him apart from his fellows. As one historian has put it, Glaber had an "instinct for dissent,"[127] for in the course of his fifty years, the troublesome monk was shown the door of monasteries in Auxerre, Champeaux, Dijon, Beze, Suze, and finally the great abbey of Cluny. But Glaber's wanderings provided him with a patchwork of perspectives that was rare for his time. He was in touch with the bush telegraph of the year 1000. No cell-bound hermit, he wrote in a chatty, over-the-garden-fence style, and if it is impossible to confirm everything that he wrote, he still provides a vivid and believable glimpse of how some people, at least, experienced the first millennium.

In the lead-up to 1000, Glaber gathered reports of a terrifying comet that had crossed the sky:

> It appeared in the month of September, not long after nightfall, and remained visible for nearly three months. It shone so brightly that its light seemed to fill the greater part of the sky, then it vanished at cock's crow. But whether it is a new star which God launches into space, or whether He merely increases the normal brightness of another star, only He can decide.... What appears established with the greatest degree of certainty is that this phenomenon in the sky never appears to men without being the sure sign of some mysterious and terrible event. And indeed, a fire soon consumed the church of St. Michael the Archangel, built on a promontory in the ocean [Mont-Saint-Michel off the coast of Brittany] which had always been the object of special veneration throughout the whole world.[128]

In conjunction with his description of the portentous comet of 989 — known today as Halley's comet — Glaber described other auguries:

> In the seventh year from the millennium . . . almost all the cities of Italy and Gaul were devastated by violent conflagrations, and Rome itself largely razed by fire. . . . As one, [the people] gave out a terrible scream and turned to rush to confess to the Prince of the Apostles.[129]

Many eminent men died around this time, recorded Glaber — though this could be said of almost any era — and there was an outbreak of heresy in Sardinia. "All this accords," wrote the monk, "with the prophecy of St. John, who said that the devil would be freed after a thousand years."[130]

Glaber had met the Devil, who appeared at the end of his bed several times. As the monk recalled from his visions, the Prince of Darkness was a shaggy, black, hunched-up figure with pinched nostrils, a goat's beard, and blubbery lips with which he whispered seditious thoughts in an attempt to subvert the holy man: "Why do you monks bother with vigils, fasts, and mortifications?" cooed Lucifer on one visit. "One day, one hour of repentance, is all you need to earn eternal bliss. . . . So why bother to rise at the sound of the bell when you could go on sleeping?"[131]

Some historians have cited this Dr. Faustus–like episode as discrediting the reliability of Glaber's testimony. But the monk's account of his vision neatly voiced the paradox which the doctrine of repentance poses to any Christian: if repentance guarantees salvation, why not enjoy a few good juicy sins before you repent? If anything, Glaber's dream indicated the reasoning of a sceptical mind — and his history did not dwell excessively on St. John's gloomy prophecies of millennial misery. After the monk's account of the natural disasters of the 990s, he moved smartly on to the year 1003:

> Just before the third year after the millennium, throughout the whole world, but especially in Italy and Gaul, men began to reconstruct churches, although for the most part the existing ones were properly built and not in the least unworthy. But it seemed as though each Christian community were aiming to surpass all others in the splendour of construction. It was as if the whole world were shaking itself free, shrugging off the burden of the past, and cladding itself everywhere in a white mantle of churches.[132]

Glaber described a world that had been holding its breath, expecting the worst. The worst had not happened, and as the monk travelled the countryside between Burgundy's great monastic houses, he had the chance to observe at firsthand the explosion of ecclesiastical stone building that marked the start of the eleventh century. It was echoed all over northern Christendom. To judge from the evidence of Anglo-Saxon England, there were teams of masons who travelled from community to community, offering package deals by which they erected parish churches to virtually Identikit plans. Their buildings must have shimmered, light and beautiful in the green medieval countryside just as Glaber described them — and so they still do.

Glaber linked his "white mantle" of new churches to a world that was making a fresh start, but thirty years later another set of anxieties loomed. Strictly speaking, the reign of Christ on earth did not begin until the death and resurrection of the Saviour, which occurred, according to the New Testament, when Jesus was thirty-three years old. So might 1033 prove to be the year when the dire predictions of the book of Revelation would be fulfilled?

> After the many prodigies which had broken upon the world before, after, and around the millennium of the Lord Christ [wrote Glaber], there were plenty of able men of penetrating intellect who foretold others, just as great, at the approach of the millennium of the Lord's Passion, and such wonders were soon manifest.[133]

Heresy broke out again around 1030 A.D., this time among the Lombards. There were horrendous famines which forced men into cannibalism, more beloved and distinguished church figures passed away, while pilgrims set off for Jerusalem in vast and unprecedented numbers. "It was believed," wrote Glaber, "that the order of the seasons and the elements . . . had fallen into perpetual chaos, and with it had come the end of mankind. . . . It could portend nothing other than the advent of the accursed Anti-Christ who, according to divine testimony, is expected to appear at the end of the world."[134]

Book IV of Glaber's *History* then described the manifestations that followed the happy passing of the 1033 "apocalypse":

At the millennial anniversary of the Passion of the Lord, the clouds cleared in obedience to Divine mercy and goodness and the smiling sky began to shine and flow gentle breezes. . . . At that point, in the region of Aquitaine, bishops, abbots, and other men devoted to holy religion first began to gather councils of the whole people. . . . When the news of these assemblies was heard, the entire populace joyfully came, unanimously prepared to follow whatever should be commanded them by the pastors of the church. A voice descending from Heaven could not have done more, for everyone was still under the effect of the previous calamity and feared the future loss of abundance.[135]

Glaber's reporting is confirmed by other sources. For several decades in the middle of the eleventh century huge crowds gathered in open fields in France to venerate relics and to swear oaths of peace. The movement was known as the "Peace of God," and economic historians have explained the phenomenon in terms of the church's wish to protect its estates in an era of petty warfare. Populist preaching whipped up feeling against lawless noblemen, and it is highly likely that some preachers may have called on millennial frettings for their purposes.

The theologian Abbo of Fleury recalled a premillennial sermon in his youth which did precisely this. A Parisian preacher had announced that "as soon as the number of a thousand years was completed, the Anti-Christ would come and the last judgement would soon follow."[136] Abbo pooh-poohed the preacher's anxieties by quoting some alternative passages of scripture, but in England the eloquent Archbishop Wulfstan of York had no reservations about invoking millennial fears. It was in 1014, when the war between Ethelred and the Danish invaders was at its bitterest, that England's greatest preacher composed his famous *Sermon of the Wolf to the English*:

> Dear Friends. . . . This world is in haste and is drawing ever closer to its end, and it always happens that the longer it lasts, the worse it becomes. And so it must ever be, for the coming of the Anti-Christ grows ever more evil because of the sins of the people, and then truly it will be grim and terrible widely in the world.[137]

Wulfstan's corruscating sermon has come down to us in written form. It was intended to be read by monks and delivered by priests from parish pulpits, but in its mesmeric passion one can almost hear the tones of the archbishop as he himself declaimed it. Even in translation, his prose rings with the compelling rhythm of a Jesse Jackson or Martin Luther King:

> The devil has deceived this people too much, and there has been little faith among men, though they speak fair words, and too many crimes have gone unchecked in the land. . . . The laws of the people have deteriorated altogether too often since Edgar died; and holy places are everywhere open to attack, and the houses of God are completely deprived of ancient rites, and stripped of all that is fitting; and religious orders have now for a long time been greatly despised; and widows are forced to marry unrighteously; and too many are reduced to poverty; and poor men are wretchedly deceived, most cruelly cheated and wholly innocent, sold out of this land far and wide into the possession of foreigners; and

through cruel injustice, children in the cradle are enslaved for petty theft widely within this nation; and the rights of freemen suppressed and the rights of slaves curtailed, and the rights of charity neglected; and, to speak most briefly, God's laws are hated and His commands despised.[138]

Preaching in 1014, Wulfstan made no reference to the anniversaries of 1000 and 1033 on which Glaber dwelt, but his words carried the same sense of crossing some awesome threshold in time. People were holding their breath in England, as Glaber described in France. Dates were not Wulfstan's concern, but the miseries of England were, and the archbishop had no doubt that the Vikings in their dragonships were acting as instruments of the Anti-Christ: "We pay them continually, and they humiliate us daily. They ravage and they burn, plunder and steal and carry off to their fleet. And lo! What other thing is clear and evident in all these events, if not the anger of God?"[139]

As the year 2000 approaches, modern historians have debated whether the concerns expressed by Glaber and Wulfstan constitute evidence that Christendom marked the first millennium as a specially significant point in time. Those who doubt the reliability of Glaber's testimony, and who explain Wulfstan's sermon solely in terms of England's sufferings at the hands of the Vikings, point to the many English wills that were composed in the 990s. These were all written with the clear and calm assumption that the world was going to continue exactly as it always had. Not a single Anglo-Saxon will or charter makes any reference to a forthcoming apocalypse, and it would certainly be wrong to imagine crowds gathering together in Engla-lond, to count down in modern style to the end of an old era and the beginning of a new.

The December drawing of the Julius Work Calendar, our final encounter with the group of nimble little figures who have laboured with such good humour month by month through the year, shows business as usual. The good folk are flailing, winnowing, and carrying away the produce of their harvest ready for next year in a basket of especially fine woven wattle, and there is every reason to believe that that is precisely how most of Engla-lond prepared for and greeted the beginning of the second millennium. Only the literate were in a position to concern themselves greatly with what would happen when the year DCCCCLXXXXVIIIJ* became a simple M, and they would have had little agreement as to the specific day and hour at which the moment should be marked: December 25th? January 1st? Lady Day?

The profusion of possible starting points for a "new year" showed how imprecisely time was divided for most people in the year 1000 — and they had heavyweight authority for their vagueness. It was ludicrous and impertinent, argued the philosopher St. Augustine of Hippo, for man to impose his own mortal calculations on the workings of God. According to the "business as usual" school of modern historians, the millennial preoccupations of Glaber and Wulfstan hold no more significance than the jeremiads of the gullible and doom-laden who agonise in every society — the medieval equivalents of believers in UFOs, the Bermuda Triangle, and the X files.

---

*999 — the Anglo-Saxons followed the older Roman style of numbering.

And yet. And yet . . . The appeal of Wulfstan's remarkable sermon derives from the power with which it captures and gives expression to the spirit of its times. Its pervading feeling of doom has a resonance that is deeper than the imagining of a single clergyman, while Ralph Glaber's history rings with the same echo. Glaber's narrative may have been colourful, but it was not concocted out of thin air. Sin, punishment, and Anti-Christ were clearly linked in these vivid contemporary visions to a common concern with a crossroad in time. The world was turning, and though it is in the nature of the world to turn, the ending of the first millennium clearly provided some people with the stimulus to contemplate that fact with extra seriousness, and to ponder the wonder and despair contained within the eternal platitude.

Down in Rome the worrying new millennium was ushered in by a worrying new Pope. A precise reading of Revelation does not predict that the world will end with the completion of a thousand years. It prophesies, rather, that the Devil will be unleashed to work his mischief, and as people looked around for evidence of where or who the Anti-Christ might be, they fixed on the Papacy and its controversial new occupant, Gerbert of Aurillac, who had taken the title of Pope Sylvester II.

Named after the small town in Aquitaine where he was born in 941 A.D., Gerbert went to Spain as a young man to explore the mathematical and scientific techniques of the Saracens, where he also dug around for the classical texts of Plato, Aristotle, and the dangerously worldly love poems of Ovid. Gerbert studied the diseases of the eye, and as a gifted musician, he built his own version of the new mechanical wind-organs. He built himself a planetarium, filled with wooden spheres, to work out the movements of the heavenly bodies. He wrote a treatise on the astrolabe. If anyone embodied the anxiety-provoking spirit of a new age, it was this clever and disputacious man who made as many enemies as Ralph Glaber, but who rose to significantly greater heights.

It was the patronage of the Ottonian dynasty which gave Gerbert his eminence. Inspired by the ambition of Otto I, the German king who sought to re-create the empire of Charlemagne and to relocate its headquarters in Rome, the Ottonians dominated the politics of Europe in the decades leading up to the millennium. Gerbert came to the attention of Otto II in one of the set-piece philosophical debates that were the heavyweight boxing championships of the time. Scholars and students would travel from all over Europe to watch these public debates, cheering on the learned contestants as they argued the pros and cons of a philosophical proposition.

Gerbert triumphed in a day-long debate at Ravenna in November 980 where his quickness of wit earned victory for the proposition that physics is a branch of mathematics, not a separate discipline in its own right. Otto II had presided over the tournament as master of ceremonies and referee, and the emperor seized on Gerbert as an intellect who could add lustre to his ambitions. The Ottonians were looking for class wherever they could get it. In the 930s Otto I had married King Athelstan's sister Edith to acquire some of the lustre of Europe's oldest royal dynasty, the house of Wessex. After Otto II's death in 983, Gerbert remained a client, adviser, and court mathematician to his successor, Otto III, only a child at his accession, and he also gave advice to the Frankish duke Hugh Capet, who made himself king of France in 987 in no small part thanks to the counsel and influence of the wily churchman.

It was small wonder that the high-powered intellect and wide-ranging political influence of Gerbert came to inspire envy and mistrust. The man must have contracted a pact with the Devil, argued his detractors, and they used Gerbert's fondness for scientific instruments and the scanning of the heavens as evidence of necromancy. Gerbert's dabbling with the ancient manuscripts which he had secured through his dealings with the infidel Saracen compounded his offence, and when, thanks to the influence of Otto III, he became Pope on the very eve of the millennium, his critics had all the proof they needed. Gerbert, the first-ever French Pope, could only have secured his throne by selling his soul, it was said. The Anti-Christ had come to power in Christendom just as St. John had prophesied.

Gerbert died only three years later, and this was taken as final confirmation of his apostasy. The Devil could not wait to reclaim his own. Legend had it that Gerbert's dying request was that his body be cut into separate pieces so that Satan could not carry him all away, and this tale was taken so seriously that six and a half centuries later, in 1648, Vatican researchers had his body exhumed. The skeleton was found intact.

When Gerbert became Pope in 999, his choice of the title Sylvester II invited deliberate comparison with the first Sylvester, who had been bishop of Rome at the time of Constantine, the earliest Christian emperor. But the feast of the first Sylvester was December 31, New Year's Eve in classical Rome, and the linking of this second Sylvester with the pagan date was more grist to the mill of his critics. The new Pope's most suspicious innovation of all was his espousing of the abacus, the exotic calculating machine which was revolutionising the arithmetic of the time. The use of Roman numerals had a paralysing effect on calculation. It was hard enough to add MCXIV to CXCIX, but to multiply one set of letters by the other was virtually impossible. The scholar Alcuin said that 9,000 should be regarded as the upper limit beyond which figuring was not possible, and when that was written out as MMMMMMMMM one could understand what he meant.

With the abacus, however, these complex calculations could be accomplished with a few flicks of the beads of a counting frame, or, more usually in western Europe, with the movement of counters on a chequered table — hence the development in England early in the second millennium of the government counting house, the exchequer. Just as conventional calculations are swallowed up by the modern microchip, so the mechanism of the abacus obliterated the need to write out figures, speeding calculation in a magical fashion. Its potential effect on the business, intellectual, and scientific processes of its time was comparable to the impact of the computer today.

The abacus was one of the new and bewildering dimensions to mathematics and general thinking which included zero and infinity. These are two of the fundamental concepts which are necessary to understand a universe that operates by logical rules of its own, rather than being the inscrutable plaything of a divine creator, and they opened the way to a new world. The flowering of all these fresh ideas lay in the future — and they did not come to England until after 1066. But thanks to Gerbert of Aurillac, the first millennium's Bill Gates, they arrived in Christendom almost exactly with the year 1000, and after their arrival, life would never be the same again.

THE ENGLISH SPIRIT

> And then there is also a need that each should under-
> stand where he came from and what he is — and what
> will become of him.
>
> — *Wulfstan, Archbishop of York from 1002 to 1023*

A GREEN AND PLEASANT ENGLAND WITH
ample space to breathe, the sound of birdsong and
church bells, the sharp smell of drifting wood-
smoke on an autumn evening — life in the year 1000 can
be evoked with some powerfully attractive images, and they
are complemented by the mesmerically beautiful treasures
that have been recovered from Anglo-Saxon churches and
archaeological sites: two delicately entwined ivory angels
from Winchester, twisting and fluttering heavenwards like
the double propeller of a sycamore seed;[140] a walrus tusk,
now in Liverpool Museum, that must have been carved
sometime very close to 1000 A.D., with two cheeky sheep
peering out from below the manger of the Christ child;[141]
and from the tomb of the great Archbishop Wulfstan,
who died in 1023 A.D., an exquisitely slender bronze cloak
pin — the very pin, presumably, with which he fastened his
vestments before mounting to the pulpit — with a minus-
cule latticework of tracery etched onto its diamond-shaped
head.[142] The craftsmanship could not be bettered today.

But then in a grave at Kingsworthy in Hampshire are
found the bones of a mother with the skeleton of her baby

still inside her, trapped on its way along her birth canal. The woman must have died in the throes of labour without relief of medicine — let alone the drastic release offered by Caesarian section, which is not recorded as being attempted in England until the sixteenth century, with no mother reported as surviving the procedure until the eighteenth.[143] Reconstruction of the Kingsworthy mother's pelvis shows it to have been narrow and constricted, while the bones of the infant are larger than average, suggesting a birthweight of nine to ten pounds.[144] So the best explanation of these remains — as for those of another tragic skeleton found in London with foetal bones inside the abdomen — is that the mother died, almost certainly of sheer exhaustion, after long hours of trying vainly to deliver a child that never had a chance of being born. Death, disease, and discomfort were daily companions in the year 1000, and living through the annual round of toil set out in the pages of the Julius Work Calendar represented a veritable triumph of the human spirit.

The simplest things were so difficult to accomplish. It took enormous time and effort to manufacture just a single coin, or to turn on a hand lathe the wooden cups that would today be produced in vast quantities by a machine. Every basic artefact represented hours of skill and effort and ingenuity, in return for a very meagre material reward. Kings and eminent churchmen lived in relative comfort, but there were no large or exaggerated profit margins for anyone. For the vast majority of ordinary people life was a struggle in even the smallest respect. Imagine wearing scratchy underwear made of coarse, hand-woven wool, since there was no cotton. Only the wealthy could afford garments of linen —

and that was woven to a texture that would be too itchy for many a modern skin. The poetry of the year 1000 celebrated the qualities of the hero, and just to survive on a day-to-day basis every man and woman had to be precisely that.

The most obvious difference between the year M and the year MM is the billions of extra people for whom this second millennium will possess some significance. Today the Jewish, Buddhist, and Moslem systems of datings still hold sway in their own cultures, where 2000 A.D. is numbered as 5760, 2544, and 1420 respectively. But the concept of the year 2000 and a new millennium has come to hold meaning for the world's many non-Christian societies, if only because of the computer systems which have turned out to be tied more intimately than intended to the system of dating popularised thirteen centuries ago by the Venerable Bede. For reasons grand, petty, and sometimes just coincidental, the culture that was developing in the misty northwest corner of Europe around the year 1000 has spread its values all over the modern world — and the drawings and Latin verses of the Julius Work Calendar provide some clues as to how and why this has happened.

The Calendar is dedicated to work and prayer. Its message is that you must labour as unquestioningly as you worship your God, and, as put into practice through the best part of the millennium that followed, this fundamental work ethic was to prove the basis of material success in England and in every other society that shared it. Already in these drawings are intimations of what was to come in the industrial West. The January ploughman is handling his massive, stall-fed oxen like so many machines. They are animals, but he is using them as enormous engines that could accomplish so much more work in so much less time than could be achieved by unassisted human labour. It was this sort of mechanical energy which produced the food surplus that, over the centuries, was to support the ever-increasing proportion of English people living in towns — and it was through the towns that mass prosperity, and mass political freedom, were eventually won.

Looking at Europe in the year 1000, there were many societies for which one might have predicted wealth and empire ahead of England — and potentially at England's expense. The ambitious Ottonian emperors controlled the old capitals of both Charlemagne and the Roman Empire. In Constantinople, the rulers of Byzantium maintained the tradition of that city's imperial greatness, while down in Spain, the Saracens threatened further conquests in the direction of the Christian kingdoms to the north. And then there were the empires based in Baghdad, Persia, and India — and further east in Korea, China, and Japan.

But all these locally dominant power structures were autocracies — and autocracy, in the long run, was not to prove the way ahead. It was inflexible and hidebound, fatally resistant to the spirit of innovation on which progress depends. The English may have looked foolish when they paid their Danegeld to the barbarous Vikings in the years around 1000, but at least they knew how to generate their money through enterprise rather than through crude conquest, and the taxes that were doubtless raised with great grumbling could only have been levied and paid over so repeatedly on some ultimate basis of popular consent.

Consent and social co-operation are among the most

difficult elements to define in any society, but they were to prove crucial for the long-term future of the English way. Sharing the technology of the plough-team was an exercise in communal organisation. Archbishop Wulfstan's description of how an agricultural estate should be run in the year 1000 depended on slave labour and was built around the authority of a lord of the manor, but that authority could only operate by respecting the rights of the community. The English described themselves as "subjects" in the year 1000, as they do today, but ten centuries of political development were to earn them rights and privileges that made them the envy of "citizens" elsewhere.

Less attractively, the English were also about to embark on a long phase in their history in which they paid signally little respect to the rights of others. Within a hundred years they were to embark on their programme of global expansion that began with the Crusades — Christendom's gleefully seized opportunity to hand back to the infidels a solid taste of the aggression from which Europe had already suffered — and England happily joined in that attack. She could thank the Normans for her warhorses, for her stone castles, and for a sharp new cutting edge to her military technology, but she financed all this with wealth that came from the wellsprings of the old Anglo-Saxon economy. Archaeology tells us of the coinage that both expressed and made possible the growing potency of English commerce, and this was to be enhanced by contemporary improvements in mathematics. The first Arabic numerals made their earliest appearance in a Western document in 976 A.D., and though centuries were to elapse before these

numerals came into common commercial use, they pointed
the way to the numeracy on which modern science, technology, business, and economics are all based.

The handful of wills and charters that have come down
to us from Anglo-Saxon England reveal another ingredient
of that society's future. The mundane precision with which
these documents describe every detail of a particular estate
boundary shows the seriousness with which the possession
of property was taken in the year 1000, and though this was
by no means unique to England, it was to prove another
ingredient in the country's future success. In the eighteenth
century Edmund Burke would argue that the sanctity of
property was the basic prerequisite of economic enterprise,
since incentive can have no meaning until society makes it
possible for property to be held securely.[145]

The ultimate guarantee of this security was a respect
for the law, the fundamental engine of healthy social
growth — the idea that no man can be above the law, least
of all lords and kings as they exercise their power. This was
already inherent in the law codes regulating English life in
the year 1000, and it helped provide this industrious society
with an extraordinarily well developed sense of national
cohesion. The concept of the nation state had yet to be
articulated, and that concept was to engender much blood-
shed and suffering, but it provided the lodestone of English
existence for the next thousand years.

As we today look forward to a millennium in which
supranational, global organisation appears a very obvious
key to the future, some may regard nationality as an out-
moded concept. But nationality was the engine of En-

gland's progress in the centuries that followed the year
1000. Archbishop Wulfstan's mesmeric sermon to his fellow countrymen was both a doom-laden lament and a clar-
ion call to England's sense of itself. Geography was one vital
factor, and language provided another, for though English
democracy, technology, and economic enterprise were to
secure many conquests in the course of the next thousand years, it was the strength and flexibility of the English language which secured the most universal conquests
of all.

The earliest documents that were written in *Englisc*
tended by their nature towards formality if they were legal
documents, and to conventional heroics if they were poems.
But one Old English poem does survive that conveys
something of the inner questioning, along with the stoic
spirit of destiny, that inspired men and women to keep on
battling with the realities of life at the turn of the first
millennium:

> *Often and again, through God's grace,*
> *Man and woman usher a child*
> *Into the world and clothe him in gay colours;*
> *They cherish him, teach him as the seasons turn*
> *Until his young bones strengthen,*
> *His limbs lengthen . . .*

Entitled "The Fortunes of Men,"[146] the poem was a medi-
tation on fate — *wyrd* in *Englisc*, literally "what will be" —
for having described the fresh and innocent joy of a young
mother and father raising their children, the anonymous
author went on to examine the different destinies that a

first-millennial child might actually encounter in the course
of its life:

> *Hunger will devour one, storm dismast another,*
> *One will be spear-slain, one hacked down in battle . . .*

"The Fortunes of Men" offered a comprehensive catalogue of the hazards that a young man — or his worrying
parents — might fear in England in the year 1000, from
falling out of a tree at apple harvest time, to a quarrel at a
feast where the drink flowed too free:

> *One will drop, wingless, from the high tree . . .*
> *One will swing from the tall gallows . . .*
> *The sword's edge will shear the life of one*
> *At the mead-bench, some angry sot*
> *Soaked with wine. His words were too hasty . . .*

But life could offer joy and achievement as well — "a
young man's ecstasy," suggested the poet, ". . . strength in
wrestling . . . skill in throwing and shooting . . . good fortune at dice . . . a devious mind for chess." Surveying the
up-side, "The Fortunes of Men" set out the earthly pleasures of which people dreamed at the turn of the first millennium, though the nature of the pleasures that the poet
envisaged for those favoured by Fate and God suggested the
workings of a distinctly male ambition. The poet's wish list
of sport, easy money, and a good time in the pub was that of
any red-blooded twentieth-century lad:

> *One will delight a gathering, gladden*
> *Men sitting at the mead-bench over their beer . . .*
> *One will settle beside his harp*

At his lord's feet, be handed treasures . . .
One will tame that arrogant wild bird,
The hawk on the fist, until the falcon
Becomes gentle; he puts jesses on it . . .

The poet left his audience with the big question: which way will your life turn — to happiness or to some living tragedy? And *wyrd*, the answer in the year 1000, was as imponderably challenging as "What Will Be" today. Only God, or Fate, could tell.

What C. S. Lewis called the "snobbery of chronology" encourages us to presume that just because we happen to have lived after our ancestors and can read books which give us some account of what happened to them, we must also know better than them. We certainly have more facts at our disposal. We have more wealth, both personal and national, better technology, and infinitely more skilful ways of preserving and extending our lives. But whether we today display more wisdom or common humanity is an open question, and as we look back to discover how people coped with the daily difficulties of existence a thousand years ago, we might also consider whether, in all our sophistication, we could meet the challenges of their world with the same fortitude, good humour, and philosophy.

Acknowledgements

This book had its origins in an idea by Danny Danziger, who picked up very little English history while studying at Harrow School. Rather more studious was his classmate Tyerman — today Dr. Christopher Tyerman, Head of History at Harrow — and we would like to thank Christopher for the historical expertise with which he has overseen our project, though the responsibility for mistakes is, of course, our own.

As working journalists, our notion was to ask the questions about everyday life and habits that conventional history books often ignore, directing our questions at some of the most eminent historians and archaeologists in the field. Christopher helped us pick them, and we would like to thank these experts for tolerating our ignorance and for sparing time to answer our questions and, in many cases, for reviewing draft versions of the manuscript. We have spent the last eighteen months in the year 1000. They have spent most of their lives there, and our debt to their knowledge and generosity is beyond measure:

Dr. Anna Abulafia, Lucy Cavendish College, Cambridge
Dr. Debby Banham, Newnham College, Cambridge
Dr. Matthew Bennett, Royal Military College, Sandhurst
Dr. Mark Blackburn, Fitzwilliam Museum, Cambridge
Dr. John Blair, Queen's College, Oxford
Professor Don Brothwell, University of York
Dr. Michelle Brown, Department of Manuscripts, British Library, London

Professor James Campbell, Worcester College, Oxford

Professor Thomas Charles-Edwards, Jesus College, Oxford

Mr. Eric Christiansen, New College, Oxford

Rev. John Cowdrey, St. Edmund Hall, Oxford

Dr. Katie Cubitt, University of York

Dr. Ken Dark, University of Reading

Professor Christopher Dyer, University of Birmingham

Dr. Richard Eales, University of Kent

Dr. Ros Faith, Wolfson College, Oxford

Richard Falkiner, coins and medals expert

Professor Richard Fletcher, University of York

Dr. Simon Franklin, Clare College, Cambridge

Dr. Richard Gameson, University of Kent

Dr. George Garnett, St. Hugh's College, Oxford

Professor John Gillingham, London School of Economics

Professor Malcolm Godden, Pembroke College, Oxford

Professor James Graham-Campbell, University College, London

Dr. Allan Hall, University of York

Dr. Richard Hall, York Archaeological Trust

Dr. David Hill, University of Manchester

Dr. Peregrine Hordern, All Souls College, Oxford

Dr. James Howard-Johnston, Corpus Christi College, Oxford

Dr. Gillian Hutchinson, Maritime Museum, Greenwich

Dr. Andrew K. G. Jones, University of Bradford and York
    Archaeological Trust

Dr. Paul Joyce , St. Peter's College, Oxford

Dr. Simon Keynes, Trinity College, Cambridge

Dr. Ken Lawson, St. Paul's School, London

Dr. Henrietta Leyser, St. Peter's College, Oxford

Dr. John Maddicott, Exeter College, Oxford

Dr. Ailsa Mainman, York Archaeological Trust

Dr. Patrick McGurk, Birkbeck College, London

Professor Henry Mayr-Harting, Christ Church, Oxford

Professor Rosamond McKitterick, Newnham College, Cambridge

Dr. Patricia Morison, All Soul's College, Oxford

Professor Janet Nelson, King's College, London

Dr. Andy Orchard, Emmanuel College, Cambridge
Dr. Christopher Page, Sidney Sussex College, Cambridge
Steve Pollington, Da Engliscan Gesidas (the English Companions)
Dr. Eric Poole and Georgina Poole, translators of classical documents
J. Kim Siddorn, Regia Anglorum
Dr. Richard Smith, Downing College, Cambridge
Professor Alfred Smyth, St. George's House, Windsor Castle
Professor Pauline Stafford, University of Huddersfield
Dr. Andrew Wathey, Royal Holloway College, London
Dr. Leslie Webster, British Library, London
Professor Christopher Wickham, University of Birmingham
Mr. Patrick Wormald, Christ Church, Oxford

All interviews were conducted by Danny Danziger, with the exception of those with Richard Falkiner, Dr. David Hill, Dr. Patrick McGurk, Dr. Patricia Morison, Steve Pollington, Dr. Eric and Georgina Poole, and J. Kim Siddorn, who were interviewed by Robert Lacey. At the British Museum, Dr. Michelle Brown was kind enough to spare time for both authors, and to let us examine the Julius Work Calendar.

We would like to give particular acknowledgement to the work of Dr. Patrick McGurk, who has carried out the most precise academic research to date on the Julius Work Calendar, and to Dr. Eric and Georgina Poole, who executed a full translation of the calendar text into modern English. Copies of this translation are available on application to the authors, c/o the publisher.

Regia Anglorum is a society whose five hundred members gather together to re-create the life and times of the Vikings, Anglo-Saxons, and other inhabitants of the British Isles in the century leading up to the Norman Conquest in 1066. For information on Regia Anglorum's forty regional branches, contact J. Kim Siddorn, 9 Durleigh Close, Bristol BS13 7NQ; e-mail: 101364.35@compuserve.com; Internet: http://www/ftech.net/~regia. We are grateful to the society's authenticity officer, Roland Williamson, for reviewing the manuscript.

The authors would like to thank for their help: the staffs of the Manuscript Room and the Reading Room of the British Library, and the photographic reproduction staff; Fionnuala Jervis, who visited the Viking Adventure in Dublin and the National Museum of Ireland on our behalf; Leonard Lewis; the staff of the London Library; Andrew and Malini Maxwell-Hyslop; the endlessly helpful staff and partners of the John Sandoe bookshop, who tracked down recondite Anglo-Saxon treatises; pruning expert Gordon Taylor; Dr. John Taylor; Dr. Penny Wallis; the staff of the Anglo-Saxon village at West Stow in Suffolk; the Jorvik Viking Centre, Coppergate, York, and the York Archaeological Trust; the Shaftesbury Museum, Dorset; Shaftesbury Abbey Museum, Dorset; the Abbey House, Malmesbury; Dorothy White.

We would also like to thank our literary agents, Jonathan Lloyd and Michael Shaw of Curtis Brown; our inspired editors at Little, Brown — Philippa Harrison in London and Bill Phillips in New York — and also Betty Power, our immensely efficient copyeditor in Boston. Thanks to Ruth Cross for her subtle and satisfying index.

It was Nina Drummond who suggested that this book be cast in the form of a calendar in order to reflect the rhythm of life in the year 1000. She has typed the manuscript, has excavated obscure books and articles, and, in the company of Osric, her faithful Anglo-Saxon springer spaniel, has visited Anglo-Saxon villages and abbeys, and got her feet wet tramping the causeway that the Vikings crossed to fight the Battle of Maldon. This book would not have been possible without her — nor without Sandi Lacey. Her contribution to the design and human concepts of the writing is stamped on every chapter.

Our other great debt is to our partners and colleagues at *Cover*, the little magazine of big words and pictures which we founded together in 1997. We started research for this book at the same moment that we started work on our first dummy issue, and the enjoyment and success of both projects owes much to the editorial and management teams who have kept producing brilliant new issues while we have been delving into the mysteries of millennial Viagra, how to charm a swarm of bees, or how to cure an Anglo-Saxon headache. This book is dedicated to them — and through them, to our loyal subscribers and readers.

Danny Danziger and Robert Lacey
November 1998

Bibliography

This bibliography lists the books and articles on which the text is based, in addition to material supplied by the interviews listed on pages 203–205. Readers stimulated to further research are warmly recommended to the most easily available paperback sourcebooks: *The Anglo-Saxon World* (Oxford University Press, 1982), translated and edited by Kevin Crossley-Holland, and Michael Swanton's *Anglo-Saxon Prose* (Everyman, 1993).

Attwater, Donald. *A New Dictionary of Saints*. Tonbridge Wells: Burns & Oates, 1993.

Baker, Peter S., and Lapidge, Michael. *Byrhtferth's Enchiridion*. London: Early English Text Society, 1995.

Banham, Debby. *Monasteriales Indicia*. Hockwold-cum-Wilton: Anglo-Saxon Books, 1991.

Banks, F. R. *English Villages*. London: Batsford, 1963.

Barber, Richard. *The Penguin Guide to Medieval Europe*. London: Penguin, 1984.

Barnes, W. *Early England and the Saxon-English*. London: John Russell Smith, 1859.

Barraclough, Geoffrey. *The Crucible of Europe*. London: Thames & Hudson, 1976.

———. ed. *Social Life in Early England*. Historical Association Essays. London: Routledge & Kegan Paul, 1960.

Beckwith, John. *Early Medieval Art*. London: Thames & Hudson, 1969.

Bede. *Ecclesiastical History of the English People.* Edited by D. H. Farmer. Translated by Leo Sherley-Price. London: Viking Penguin, 1955.

Brent, Peter. *The Viking Saga.* London: Weidenfeld and Nicholson, 1975.

Britnell, Richard H. *The Commercialisation of English Society.* Manchester: Manchester University Press, 1996.

Brooke, Christopher. *Europe in the Central Middle Ages, 962–1154.* London: Longmans, 1964.

———. *The Structure of Medieval Society.* London: Thames & Hudson, 1971.

Brooke, Christopher, and Brooke, Rosalind. *Popular Religion in the Middle Ages.* London: Thames and Hudson, 1984.

Brown, Michelle P. *Anglo-Saxon Manuscripts.* London: British Library, 1991.

Brown, Ron. *Beekeeping — A Seasonal Guide.* London: Batsford, 1992.

Cahill, Thomas. *How the Irish Saved Civilisation.* New York: Nan A. Talese/Doubleday, 1996.

Campbell, James (with Eric John and Patrick Wormald). *The Anglo-Saxons.* Oxford: Phaidon, 1982.

Camporesi, Piero, "Bread of Dreams," *History Today,* Vol. 39, April 1989.

Cheney, C. R., ed. *Handbook of Dates for Students of English History.* Cambridge: Cambridge University Press, 1991.

Claiborne, Robert. *Climate, Man and History.* London: Angus & Robertson, 1973.

Crook, John, ed. *Winchester Cathedral: Nine Hundred Years, 1093–1993.* Chichester: Dean & Chapter of Winchester Cathedral in conjunction with Phillimore, 1993.

Crossley-Holland, Kevin, ed. *The Anglo-Saxon World — An Anthology.* Oxford: Oxford University Press, 1982.

Daumas, Maurice. *A History of Technology & Invention,* Vol. 1. London: John Murray, 1980.

Davis, Ralph H. C. *The Normans and Their Myth.* London: Thames & Hudson, 1976.

———. *The Medieval Warhorse.* London: Thames & Hudson, 1989.

Deegan, Marilyn, and Scragg, D. G., eds. *Medicine in Early Medieval England*. Manchester: Centre for Anglo-Saxon Studies, 1987.

Derry, T. K., and Williams, Trevor. *A Short History of Technology from the Earliest Times to A.D. 1900*. Oxford: Clarendon Press, 1960.

Diamond, Jared. *Guns, Germs and Steel*. London: Vintage, 1998.

Drummond, J. C., and Wilbraham, Anne. *The Englishman's Food*. London: Pimlico, 1991.

Duby, Georges. *L'An Mil*. Paris: Editions Gallimard/Julliard, 1980.

Edson, Evelyn. *Mapping Time and Space: How Medieval Mapmakers Viewed Their World*. London: British Library, 1997.

Erdoes, Richard. *A.D. 1000: Living on the Brink of Apocalypse*. San Francisco: Harper & Row, 1988.

Faith, Rosamond. *The English Peasantry and the Growth of Lordship*. London: Leicester University Press, 1997.

Farmer, David. *Oxford Dictionary of Saints*. Oxford: Oxford University Press, 1997.

Fell, Christine. *Women in Anglo-Saxon England*. London: British Museum, 1984.

Fichtenau, Heinrich. *Living in the Tenth Century*. Chicago: University of Chicago Press, 1991.

Finberg, H. P. R. *The Formation of England 550-1042*. London: Hart-Davis, MacGibbon, 1974.

Fletcher, Richard. *The Conversion of Europe*. London: HarperCollins, 1997.

Flint, Valerie I. J. *The Rise of Magic in Early Medieval Europe*. Oxford: Clarendon Press, 1991.

Focillon, Henri. *The Year 1000*. Evanston, New York: Harper Torchbooks, 1971.

France, John, ed. and trans. *Rodulfus Glaber Opera*. Oxford: Clarendon Press, 1989.

Gilbert, Martin. *Atlas of British History*. London: J. M. Dent, 1993.

Griffiths, Bill. *Aspects of Anglo-Saxon Magic*. Hockwold-cum-Wilton: Anglo-Saxon Books, 1996.

———. *The Battle of Maldon*. Hockwold-cum-Wilton: Anglo-Saxon Books, 1991.

——. *An Introduction to Early English Law*. Hockwold-cum-Wilton: Anglo-Saxon Books, 1995.

Hagen, Anne. *A Handbook of Anglo-Saxon Food: Processing and Consumption*. Pinner: Anglo-Saxon Books, 1992.

——. *A Second Handbook of Anglo-Saxon Food and Drink: Production and Distribution*. Hockwold-cum-Wilton: Anglo-Saxon Books, 1995.

de Hamel, Christopher. *Medieval Craftsmen — Scribes and Illuminators*. London: British Museum Press, 1992.

Heaney, Seamus, trans. "Beowulf," Books Section, *Sunday Times*, London, 26 July 1998.

Henson, Donald. *A Guide to Late Anglo-Saxon England from Alfred to Eadgar II*. Hockwold-cum-Wilton: Anglo-Saxon Books, 1998.

Herbert, Kathleen. *Looking for the Lost Gods of England*. Hockwold-cum-Wilton: Anglo-Saxon Books, 1994.

——. *Peace-Weavers and Shield-Maidens: Women in Early English Society*. Hockwold-cum-Wilton: Anglo-Saxon Books, 1997.

Herzfeld, George. *An Old English Martyrology*. London: Kegan Paul, Trench, Trubner for the Early English Text Society, reprinted 1997.

Hill, David. *An Atlas of Anglo-Saxon England*. Oxford: Basil Blackwell, 1981.

——. "A Handful of Grit — Anglo-Saxon Bee-Keeping," *Beekeeper's Quarterly*, Summer 1994, p. 28.

——. "The Crane and the Gyrfalcon in Anglo-Saxon England," *Medieval Life*, 1994.

Hooke, Della, ed. *Anglo-Saxon Settlements*. Oxford: Basil Blackwell, 1988.

Hoskins, W. G. *The Making of the English Landscape*. London: Pelican, 1970.

Howarth, David. *1066: The Year of the Conquest*. London: Penguin, 1981.

Hyland, Ann. *The Medieval Warhorse from Byzantium to the Crusades*. Dover, New Hampshire: Allan Sutton Publishing, 1994.

Johnson, Hugh. *The World Atlas of Wine*. London: Mitchell Beazley, 1971.

Jones, Gwyn. *The Vikings*. London: Folio Society, 1997.

Jones, Peter Murray. *Medieval Medicine in Illuminated Manuscripts*. London: British Library, 1998.

Kemble, John. *Anglo-Saxon Runes*. Pinner: Anglo-Saxon Books, 1991.

Landes, David. *The Wealth and Poverty of Nations.* London: Little, Brown, 1998.

Lang, James. *Anglo-Saxon Sculpture.* Aylesbury: Shire Publications, 1988.

Langland, William. *Piers the Ploughman.* Translated by J. F. Goodridge. London: Viking Penguin, 1959.

Lash, Jennifer. *On Pilgrimage.* London: Bloomsbury, 1998.

Latouche, Robert. *The Birth of Western Economy.* London: Methuen, 1961.

Leyser, Henrietta. *Medieval Women: A Social History of Women in England 450–1500.* London: Phoenix, 1996.

Leyser, Karl. *Communications and Power in Medieval Europe.* London and Rio Grande, Ohio: Hambledon Press, 1994.

Manchester, William. *A World Lit Only by Fire.* Boston: Little, Brown, 1992.

Mays, Simon. *The Archaeology of Human Bones.* London: Routledge, 1998.

McCrum, Robert, MacNeil, Robert, and Cran, William. *The Story of English.* London: Faber & Faber, 1992.

McGurk, Patrick, et al. *An Eleventh Century Anglo-Saxon Illustrated Miscellany: British Library Cotton Tiberius B. V. Part I.* Copenhagen: Early English Manuscripts in Facsimile, 1983.

McGurk, Patrick. "The Metrical Calendar of Hampson," *Analecta Bollandia*, 1986, Tome 104, Fasc. 1–2, pp. 79–125.

Morant, G. M. "A First Study of the Craniology of England and Scotland from Neolithic to Early Historic Times, with Special Reference to the Anglo-Saxon Skulls in London Museums," *Biometrika*, Vol. 18, 1926.

Moss, H. St. L. B. *The Birth of the Middle Ages, 395–814.* Oxford: Oxford University Press, 1961.

Murray, Alexander. *Reason and Society in the Middle Ages.* Oxford: Clarendon Press, 1978.

Ohler, Norbert. *The Medieval Traveller.* Woodbridge: Boydell Press, 1989.

Paor, Liam de. *Ireland and Early Europe.* Dublin: Four Courts Press, 1997.

Pearson, Karl, and Davin, Adelaide. "On the Biometric Constants of the Human Skull," *Biometrika*, Vol. 16, 1924.

Phillips, Fr. Andrew. *The Hallowing of England*. Hockwold-cum-Wilton: Anglo-Saxon Books, 1994.

Pollington, Stephen. *The English Warrior from Earliest Times to 1066*. Hockwold-cum-Wilton: Anglo-Saxon Books, 1996.

———. *An Introduction to the Old-English Language and Its Literature*. Hockwold-cum-Wilton: Anglo-Saxon Books, 1994.

———. *Wordcraft: Wordhoard and Wordlists*. Hockwold-cum-Wilton: Anglo-Saxon Books, 1993.

Porter, John. *Anglo-Saxon Riddles*. Hockwold-cum-Wilton: Anglo-Saxon Books, 1995.

Porter, Roy. *The Greatest Benefit to Mankind*. London: HarperCollins, 1997.

Postan, Michael M. *Essays on Medieval Agriculture and General Problems of the Medieval Economy*. Cambridge: Cambridge University Press, 1973.

Power, Eileen. *Medieval People: A Study of Communal Psychology*. London: Penguin, 1937.

Pulsiano, Phillip, and Treharne, Elaine. *Anglo-Saxon Manuscripts and Their Heritage*. Aldershot and Brookfield, Vermont: Ashgate, 1998.

Rodger, N. A. M. *The Safeguard of the Sea — A Naval History of Britain*. London: HarperCollins, 1997.

Rodrigues, Louis J. *Anglo-Saxon Verse Charms, Maxims and Heroic Legends*. Pinner: Anglo-Saxon Books, 1993.

Rollason, David. *Saints and Relics in Anglo-Saxon England*. Oxford: Basil Blackwell, 1989.

Rosener, Werner. *Peasants in the Middle Ages*. Cambridge: Polity Press, 1992.

Sawyer, Peter H., ed. *Anglo-Saxon Charters: An Annotated List and Bibliography*. London: Royal Historical Society, 1968.

Smith, Alan. *Sixty Saxon Saints*. Hockwold-cum-Wilton: Anglo-Saxon Books, 1994.

Southern, R. W. *The Making of the Middle Ages*. London: Arrow Books, 1959.

Stafford, Pauline. *Queen Emma and Queen Edith*. Oxford: Blackwell, 1997.

Staniland, Kay. *Medieval Craftsmen — Embroiderers*. London: British Museum Press, 1991.

Stratton, John M. *Agricultural Records, A.D. 220-1968*. London: John Baker, 1969.

Swanton, Michael, trans. and ed. *The Anglo-Saxon Chronicle*. London: J. M. Dent, 1997.

———. *Anglo-Saxon Prose*. London: J. M. Dent, 1993.

Sweeney, Del, ed. *Agriculture in the Middle Ages*. Philadelphia: University of Pennsylvania Press, 1995.

Thompson, Damian. *The End of Time*. London: Minerva, 1997.

Thorndike, Lynn. *A History of Magic and Experimental Science*. New York: Macmillan, 1923.

Tite, Colin. *The Manuscript Library of Sir Robert Cotton: The Panizzi Lectures*. London: British Library, 1993.

Walsh, Michael. *A Dictionary of Devotions*. Tonbridge Wells: Burns & Oates, 1993.

Werner, Alex, ed. *London Bodies: The Changing Shape of Londoners from Prehistoric Times to the Present Day*. London: Museum of London, 1998.

Wheeler, A., and Jones, A. K. G. *Fishes*. Cambridge: Cambridge University Press, 1989.

Whitelock, Dorothy. *Anglo-Saxon Wills*. Cambridge: Cambridge University Press, 1930.

———. *The Beginnings of English Society*. London: Penguin, 1952.

———. *English Historical Documents, c. 500–1042*. London: Eyre & Spottiswoode, 1955.

Wormald, Francis, ed. *English Kalendars before A.D. 1100*. London: Henry Bradshaw Society, 1934.

Wormald, Patrick, ed. (with D. Bullough and R. Collins). *Ideal and Reality in Frankish and Anglo-Saxon Society*. Oxford: Basil Blackwell, 1983.

Source Notes

The Julius Work Calendar can be studied at the British Library in London, subject to the rules and conditions of access to the Manuscript Room. It is catalogued as Cotton MS Julius A.VI. See the works of Patrick McGurk listed in the bibliography on page 207 for the latest published academic transcript and analysis of the document, and also Baker and Lapidge for a transcription and translation of the text at the head of the calendar page. Dr. David Hill of the University of Manchester has prepared a most important illustrated, but as yet unpublished, analysis of the calendar from the point of view of Anglo-Saxon farming techniques, *The Turning Year*. In addition to the ideas and themes suggested by our interviews with the experts listed on pages 203–205, important details in the text come from the following sources, whose full details can be found in the bibliography:

1. See Tite, p. 79, for a description of Sir Robert Cotton's library.
2. Fell, p. 21.
3. See Werner, p. 108, for a table of London body heights over the centuries, based on excavations going back to prehistoric times. This shows, for example, that the average Saxon male body height was 5′8″, as compared to the modern average of 5′9″ (and a Victorian male average of 5′5½″). The table also shows that, at 5′4¼″, the average Saxon female was actually taller than the modern female Londoner, whose average height is 5′3¾″. The equivalent height for the female Victorian was 5′1¼″.

4. Ibid.

5. Swanton, *Anglo-Saxon Prose*, pp. 174, 175.

6. Derry and Williams, p. 57; Daumas, pp. 468-470.

7. Bede, p. 186.

8. Ibid., p. 189.

9. *Encyclopaedia Britannica*, Macropaedia, vol. 3, pp. 595 ff., Calendar.

10. Farmer, pp. 339, 340.

11. Herzfeld, p. x.

12. Bede, p. 75.

13. Phillips, p. 40.

14. *Aelfric's Lives of the Saints*, quoted in Brooke, *Popular Religion*, p. 37.

15. Ibid.

16. Whitelock, *Anglo-Saxon Wills*, p. 39. Aelfflaed was the widow of Byrhtnoth, hero of the Battle of Maldon (see p. 76).

17. Ibid., p. 55.

18. Whitelock, *English Historical Documents*, p. 536.

19. It is a commonplace of archaeological research that human brain volumes have not altered significantly since early historical times. See the articles by Morant and by Pearson in *Biometrika*.

20. Heaney, lines 216–222.

21. Johnson, p. 26.

22. McCrum, p. 55. It must be presumed that significant numbers of Britons remained in their homes and became assimilated with the invaders, but there is no way of quantifying how many.

23. Ibid., p. 58.

24. Our thanks to Stephen Pollington for supplying these examples of Old English and Norse dialogue.

25. McCrum, p. 71.

26. Swanton, *Anglo-Saxon Chronicle*, pp. 106, 109.

27. Ibid., entries for 962, 973 and 978 A.D.

28. McCrum, pp. 70, 71.

29. Daumas, p. 489.

30. Whitelock, *Anglo-Saxon Wills*, pp. 111, 112.

31. Crossley-Holland, p. 262.

32. Finberg, p. 220.

33. Ibid., p. 224. The tract is called the *Gerefa*.

34. Crossley-Holland, p. 261.
35. Aelfric, "Sermon on the Sacrifice of Easter Day," in Swanton, *Anglo-Saxon Prose*, pp. 149–152.
36. Langland, p. 81.
37. Swanton, *Anglo-Saxon Chronicle*, pp. 121 ff.
38. Hagen, *Handbook*, p. 107.
39. Ibid., p. 112.
40. Bede, p. 226.
41. Hagen, *Handbook*, p. 109.
42. Hagen, *Second Handbook*, p. 93.
43. Ibid., p. 163.
44. Whitelock, *Anglo-Saxon Wills*, p. 65.
45. Hagen, *Second Handbook*, pp. 230, 231.
46. Riddle from the Exeter Book, cited in Hagen, *Second Handbook*, p. 233.
47. *Beowulf*, in Crossley-Holland, p. 89.
48. Hooke, p. 207.
49. Whitelock, *English Historical Documents*, p. 829.
50. Andrew Pulsiano, "The Ghost of Asser," in Pulsiano and Treharne, p. 255.
51. Daumas, p. 506.
52. Finberg, p. 76.
53. Ibid., p. 190.
54. Pollington, *English Warrior*, Appendix III.
55. Swanton, *Anglo-Saxon Prose*, pp. 181, 182.
56. *Anglo-Saxon Chronicle*, quoted in Finberg, pp. 183, 184.
57. Swanton, *Anglo-Saxon Prose*, p. 175.
58. Derry and Williams, p. 90.
59. Hill, "Towns as Structures and Functioning Communities," in Hooke, p. 207.
60. Whitelock, *Beginnings*, p. 116.
61. Ibid., p. 129.
62. Ibid., p. 132.
63. Ibid., p. 133.
64. Bede, p. 359.
65. Southern, p. 44.

66. Ibid., pp. 34, 35.

67. Swanton, *Anglo-Saxon Prose*, p. 173.

68. Rodger, p. xxiii.

69. Ibid., pp. 4–16.

70. Alfred's *Metres of Boethius*, metre 20, lines 161–175, cited in Griffiths, *Anglo-Saxon Magic*, p. 236.

71. Robert Worth Frank, Jr., in Sweeney, p. 227.

72. Camporesi, p. 18.

73. Gilbert, p. 15.

74. Quoted by Rose Graham in Barraclough, *Social Life*, p. 74.

75. Banham, *Monasteriales Indicia*. All the following references are taken from this lucid and illuminating book, which includes a set of illustrations.

76. McGurk, "Metrical Calendar," p. 88.

77. Quoted in Hagen, *Second Handbook*, p. 363.

78. Swanton, *Anglo-Saxon Prose*, p. 174.

79. Hagen, *Handbook*, p. 20.

80. Hoskins, p. 81.

81. Fichtenau, p. 272.

82. Power, p. 108.

83. Fell, p. 146.

84. Griffiths, *Anglo-Saxon Magic*, p. 58.

85. Ibid., p. 65.

86. Jones, *Medieval Medicine*, p. 39.

87. Swanton, *Anglo-Saxon Prose*, p. 263.

88. Power, p. 24.

89. *De Temporum Ratione*, chapter 35, cited in Griffiths, *Anglo-Saxon Magic*, p. 66.

90. Bald's Leechbook, I 72, quoted in Swanton, *Anglo-Saxon Prose*, p. 259.

91. Quoted in Griffiths, *Anglo-Saxon Magic*, p. 66.

92. Bokonyi, "Stockbreeding and Herding in Medieval Europe," in Sweeney, p. 53.

93. Hagen, *Second Handbook*, p. 49.

94. Ibid.

95. Hagen, *Handbook*, p. 99.

96. Daumas, p. 276.
97. Derry and Williams, p. 67.
98. Old High German charm, quoted in Power, pp. 23, 24.
99. Rodrigues, p. 151.
100. Hill, "A Handful of Grit."
101. Claiborne, pp. 349–364.
102. *De Natura Rerum*, chapter 36, cited in Griffiths, *Anglo-Saxon Magic*, p. 230.
103. *De Tonitruis Libellus*, cited in Griffiths, *Anglo-Saxon Magic*, pp. 230–231.
104. Swanton, *Anglo-Saxon Chronicle*, 855 A.D.
105. Herbert, *Lost Gods*, p. 15.
106. Power, p. 23.
107. Herbert, *Lost Gods*, p. 20.
108. Bede, p. 76.
109. Ibid., p. 133.
110. Hill, "The Crane and the Gyrfalcon."
111. Howarth, p. 175.
112. Crossley-Holland, p. 241.
113. Porter, *Riddles*, p. 67.
114. Fell, p. 17.
115. Swanton, *Anglo-Saxon Chronicle*, 913 A.D.
116. Fell, p. 109.
117. Bede, p. 245.
118. Fell, p. 109.
119. Ibid., p. 126.
120. Ibid., p. 57.
121. Whitelock, *English Historical Documents*, p. 426.
122. Fell, p. 64.
123. Ibid., p. 47.
124. Ibid., pp. 57–59.
125. Leyser, p. 49.
126. Fell, p. 59.
127. Focillon, p. 64.
128. France, p. 111.
129. Ibid., p. 75.

130. Ibid., p. 93.

131. Ibid., p. 216.

132. Ibid., pp. 115, 117.

133. Ibid., p. 171.

134. Ibid., pp. 193, 205.

135. Thompson, pp. 47, 48.

136. Focillon, p. 54.

137. *Sermo Lupi ad Anglos*, opening paragraph, translated by Dr. Andy Orchard.

138. Crossley-Holland, pp. 294–295.

139. Ibid., p. 297.

140. Reproduced in Campbell, p. 196.

141. Ibid., p. 197.

142. Ibid., p. 201.

143. Porter, Roy, pp. 231, 277.

144. Deegan and Scragg, p. 17.

145. Landes, p. 32. See the opening chapters of this stimulating book for a wider discussion of these themes.

146. Crossley-Holland, p. 304.

Index